PARTICIPATORY MANAGEMENT OF NATURAL RESOURCES

About the Author

V. Ragupathy is a Reader in Department of Development Administration and Political Science at Gandhigram Rural Institute (Deemed University), Tamil Nadu, India. He is also the Associate Coordinator of Institute's Rajiv Gandhi Chair for Panchayati Raj Studies.

Dr. Ragupathy has served many high level committees of the Government of Tamil Nadu, State Planning Commission and various development agencies. He is also engaged in several research projects, supported by DANIDA and Ford Foundation.

PARTICIPATORY MANAGEMENT OF NATURAL RESOURCES

Irrigation Tanks in Panchayats

V. RAGUPATHY
Gandhigram Rural Institute (Deemed University)
Gandhigram, Tamil Nadu (India)

CONCEPT PUBLISHING COMPANY, NEW DELHI-110059

ISBN: 81-8069-080-6

First Published 2004

Published and Printed by
Ashok Kumar Mittal
Concept Publishing Company
A/15-16, Commercial Block, Mohan Garden
NEW DELHI-110059

Phones : 25351460, 25351794
Fax : 091-11-25357103
E-mail : publishing@conceptpub.com

PREFACE

Participatory management of natural resources was central to the culture of rural India through local community organizations. Even today the culture of participatory management of resources like water, forest and fisheries is in practice in many parts of the country. Particularly in the management of water resouces, well established based systems function successfully. But gradually such systems are eroded due to various reasons. State policy, market process, population growth and modernization are some of the major factors which influence the functioning of participatory systems. 73rd Constitutional Amendment Act is a major step towards the establishment of an institutional arrangement for participatory management of natural resources. It provides a hope for revival of participatory culture in rural areas. It also has inbuilt systems to protect gender and social justice in the process of participation. This a major development in empowering weaker section in the rural political structure.

Apart from development of Panchayati Raj Institutions, many instutitonal reforms are taking place at the grassroots level. The need for the involvement of stake holders in the decision-making and execution process is often highlighted. For this purpose experiments on different types of participatory institutional models are going on. Users organizations, self help groups and joint management groups have been promoted in different sectors of development. At many places these models have worked well and successful models have been replicated. Comparing the working of different types of participatory management practices is always useful for theorization. Success has to be objectively evaluated by fixing suitable indicators. Efficiency, equity and sustainability are the three important requirements for any participatory institutions to achieve success.

After 73rd Constitutional Amendment Act Panchayati Raj

Institutions are expected to deliver a wide range of activities related to the twenty-nine items of work listed in the Eleventh Schedule of Indian Constitution and more than ten items are directly related to natural resource management. But real devolution of power to panchayats are yet to take place in most of the states and panchayats are not able to make much progress in the management of natural resources.

In Tamil Nadu irrigation tanks play a critical role in agriculture and rural economy. For generations, community based institutions were able to manage irrigation tanks with the support and participation of the rural community. During the colonial rule the irrigation tanks were brought under the control of the public works department. After independence rain fed tanks with less than 100 acres of irrigated area were transferred to the management of panchayati raj institutions and panchayats are expected to maintain these tanks with people's participation. But in reality panchayats could not manage the tanks due to variety of problems. When the formal institutions like panchayats do not facilitate community participation for the management of critical resources like water, depending on the significance of the resources in the life of the people, community tries to use alternative methods and systems. In few areas of Tamil Nadu, where people depend on irrigation tanks for their survival, they have come forward to join together to manage irrigation tanks. Depending on the local context people select their own systems of management. Mostly community based irrigation systems are bound by tradition and customs. The case based social structures in the rural areas play a critical role in the functioning of such system. But in some places people are able to develop modern management systems based on the principles of equity, efficiency and sustainability. A remarkable level of transparency and accountability is maintained. Contrary to the popular belief, in many cases these community organizations are able to include hitherto marginalised groups like Scheduled Caste in the process of governance. These institutions are also able to understand the significance of social development issues and undertake activities related to primary education, health, sanitation, consumer protection and environment.

One cannot come to a general conclusion based on such cases and there is no need for any romantic bias towards such grassroot systems. But at the same time learning from such experiments of the community will help the policy makers while designing appropriate systems. A pluralistic approach to institutional development for participatory resource management must be given sufficient attention. The process of decentralization must give sufficient space for the community to design their local institutions based on the local needs. This is one of the major deficiencies of the decentralization process taking place in countries like India.

This study has analysed the management model evolved by the community over the years in managing the natural resources especially irrigation tanks in the backdrop established theories. It is the outcome of my research programme undertaken for the award of a doctoral degree.

The purpose of this work is to give a comprehensive picture of the complex and variegated process of peoples participation in the natural resource management and it's different manifestations. It wants to stimulate interest in the subject and provoke further research in the area with better methods and richer data.

V. RAGUPATHY

ACKNOWLEDGEMENTS

I sincerely thank my Supervisor Dr. G. Palanithurai, Rajiv Gandhi Chair Research Professor in Panchayati Raj Studies, Gandhigram Rural Institute—Deemed University, for his consistent and constant advise in shaping my thesis. Dr. G. Palanithurai organised training programme for local body leaders which facilitated my interaction with hundreds of elected leaders of the Panchayats of seven districts of the Tamil Nadu and during these periods I gained much insights in those issues.

Dr. A.K. Gupta, Professor, Indian Institute of Management, Ahmedabad, a leading Scholar in the field of Common Property Resource Management helped me by providing adequate literature in this field. His advises were valuable for my research work.

My thanks to Dr. M.A. Jeyaraju, Dean Faculty of English, Gandhigram Rural Institute for his careful perusal of the manuscript. Dr. R. Jothiprakash, Dr. M.P. Boraian, Dr. S. Lakshmi and Dr. S. Narayanasamy, helped me to finalyse my thesis by giving valuable suggestions and for which I express my thanks to them.

Mr. M. Gurusamy, Research Assistant in Rajiv Gandhi Chair for Panchayati Raj Studies helped me in data collection and without his help I could not have collected the needed field data which were confidential in nature from the perception of the Local Community Organisations.

My sincere thanks to my Colleagues and all the Staff Members in the Department.

V. RAGUPATHY

CONTENTS

ABBREVIATIONS

BC	—	Backward Class
DRDA	—	District Rural Development Agency
FC	—	Forward Class
LCK	—	Local Community Knowledge
LCO	—	Local Community Organisation
PRA	—	Participatory Rural Appraisal
PWD	—	Public Works Department
SC	—	Scheduled Caste

LIST OF TABLES

LIST OF FIGURES AND PLATES

FIGURES

PLATES

1

INTRODUCTION

People's participation in the development process has been recognised as a major factor in determining the destiny of the people. In both the developing and the developed countries, it has been emphasised that people's participation has been steadily on the increase in determining development targets and goals. In India, it is all the more important that people's participation is ensured in conserving the natural resources since the resources are being depleted fast to make profit. There is a potential danger of the community failing even to sustain their life unless the natural resources are properly maintained. In India, especially in the rural areas, the development process of the people is fully determined by the people's participation in utilising the natural resources and, more particularly, in conservation, management and enrichment of common natural resources.[1] For the maintenance of natural resources such as irrigation tanks, ponds, grazing lands, fisheries, waste land, trees and forests, the participation of the local people is considered the most important requirement. People can participate as individuals or in groups in the maintenance of natural resources. It will be more effective, useful and sustainable, if their participation is institutionalised legitimately at the local level. Institutionalisation is a fundamental requirement for effective participation. This is phenomenon that researchers have observed in recent years while investigating the management of Common Property Resources.

Statement of the Problem

Indian villages have had a rich tradition of self governance and participatory management of community resources. After Independence, initiatives were taken to establish rural local self government and facilitate people's participation in the development process. Article 40 of the Indian Constitution says, "The state shall take steps to organise village panchayats and endow them with such powers and authority as may be necessary to enable them to function as units of self government".[2] The Community Development Programme was launched in the year 1952 as a movement for development with the active participation of the community in the process of development. But, after a few years, it was found that, instead of being a people's programme, it was becoming more and more a government programme. The Balwantarai Mehta Committee reviewed the programme and suggested that the panchayati raj has to be institutionalised to ensure people's participation in the development process at the grassroot level. Based on the recommendations of the committee, many states enacted Panchayat Acts and established panchayati raj institutions. The Madras Panchayat Act, 1958 was enacted in Tamil Nadu (then it was Madras State) and attempts were made to decentralise power to lower level institutions to facilitate people's participation. But, after a few years of initial enthusiasm, the process of decentralisation in Tamil Nadu and many other states started declining.

The 73rd Constitutional Amendment Act, passed in the year 1992, gave a fillip to the panchayati raj system by conferring constitutional status on it. The Act considers panchayats as institutions of self governance and wants them to prepare plans and implement them for economic development and social justice on matters included in the eleventh schedule of the Constitution. Out of the twenty-nine items listed in the eleventh schedule, ten are related to the management of natural resources in rural areas. In this context, the Gram Sabha can ensure direct participation of the people in planning and implementation as envisaged by the 73rd Constitutional Amendment Act. The Tamil Nadu Panchayat Act ,1958 also included many sections on the functions of panchayati raj institutions in participatory management of natural resources like irrigation tanks in rural areas. The Tamil Nadu Panchayat Act, 1994 has retained most of such functions. The Tamil Nadu Panchayat Act, 1994 clearly says that the panchayati raj institutions are self governing and participatory institutions.

But studies have pointed out that, despite their legal powers, the panchayats are not able to effectively enforce any regulation on the use and management of such resources or ensure people's participation. The failure of the panchayats has led to the conversion of these useful common resources into overused, exploited, neglected and mismanaged resources, which has been termed the "tragedy of commons". Scholars have pointed out that people are seeking alternative organisations to manage such common resources for the benefits of the community. Due to the importance of these resources in their life, people in the rural areas are able to join together to establish a collective management system through informally evolved community organisations. In some pockets of Tamil Nadu such local community organisations are able to ensure effective people's participation in the management of the resources without state support. In some of the districts of Tamil Nadu, irrigation tanks play a crucial role in shaping the life of the people. Small rain-fed irrigation tanks have been entrusted to panchayats for management by the government. But, in most cases, the panchayats are not able to ensure people's participation in the management of the irrigation tanks, even though the panchayats are legally expected to do so. However, in some areas of Tamil Nadu, local community organisations are able to ensure people's participation in the management of irrigation tanks. A cursory glance at the available literature and theories on the area discussed above indicates the need to undertake a comparative study of the ability of these two institutional arrangements in ensuring people's participation in the management of panchayat irrigation tanks. People's perception of these two types of institutions as facilitators of people's participation in the management of panchayat irrigation tanks is the focus of this study. This study attempts to investigate people's perception of the ability of these two institutions (panchayats and local community organisations) to provide assurance to the people and to facilitate their participation in the management of irrigation tanks.

Review of Literature

Panchayati Raj Institutions and People's Participation in Collective Action for the Management of Common Property Resources

Panchayati raj institutions (rural local governments in India) are envisaged as self governing institutions of the people in rural areas by the Constitution of India. Especially after the enactment of the 73rd Constitutional Amendment Act by the Indian Parliament, the role of the panchayati raj as an institution of people's participation for self governance is widely accepted. Many of the crucial resources like rural irrigation systems, unreserved forests, grazing lands, water bodies and fisheries are entrusted to the panchayati raj institutions. These resources are essential for the survival of the rural people in general and the weaker sections in particular. Landless labourers, women, artisans, socially marginalised people, agricultural labourers and shepherds depend on these resources for their livelihood to some extent. Farming and cattle rearing in villages need proper maintenance of these resources. Most people in rural areas draw their fuel, fodder and water needs from these resources.

Some of the studies of scholars on common property resources in the context of panchayati raj institutions are very useful in further research in the area and they are discussed here. Jodha studied 82 villages in twenty-one districts scattered in seven major states in India.[3] He found that the common property resources are declining in many parts of the country and people's participation is affected by many factors. To a great extent, 'management systems decline' is considered to be responsible for the declining trend in people's participation. Jodha regards this phenomenon as a side effect of certain institutional reforms such as the introduction of the panchayati raj system and land reforms. According to Jodha, the management of common property resources must be free from the control of the formal panchayati raj system to facilitate people's participation in their upkeep. Jodha argues that, in spite of their legal powers, the village panchayats are generally unable to enforce any regulation on the use of common property resources among the people of the village. The dependence of the elected leaders on the voters compels them to avoid unpopular steps like enforcing users' obligation on the people.[4]

Jodha also argues that the panchayati raj institutions have greatly undermined the informal authority of the traditional leaders, who could control and regulate the behaviour of the villagers in relation to common property resources. According to Jodha, in some places, panchayati raj institutions are dominated by elected leaders who do not have a stake or interest in the common property resources, but the panchayats rarely miss any opportunity to seek government grants in the name of development of common property resources.

Jodha also makes a disturbing observation on the role of the panchayati raj institutions in the management of common property resources. The inefficiency and default of the panchayati raj institutions in enforcing the regulations relating to the use of common property resources turn them into open access resources. To Jodha, users' groups of stake holders are better equipped to manage common property resources than the panchayati raj institutions.

Jodha's argument is supported by Gupta. In his study on traditional forms of cooperation and modern organisations, he discusses the problems of modern organisations (like village cooperatives and panchayati raj institutions) in ensuring people's participation. Institutions are formed without taking the local realities and the cultural context into consideration and so they may not be able to succeed in motivating the people. The cost-benefit factors alone are not sufficient for the success of an organisation working among the people. Culture and tradition cannot be ignored and most of the modern organisations are not able to win the confidence of the people because of the above mentioned two factors.[5]

Brara, in his study of collective management of common pastures in dry regions of North India, found that, in spite of the presence of panchayati raj institutions, in places where traditional systems prevail in which village elders have authority, people are still able to join together to collectively protect their common pastures effectively and independently. Brara found that, in other places where such traditional system do not have authority, the scope for collective management of common pastures in very limited.[6]

Wade, in his study of the common property irrigation system in Kottapalle Village in Andhra Pradesh, points out the limitations of the statutory panchayat in bringing people together for a collective good.[7] He finds that the traditional council of village elders plays a significant role in ensuring people's participation in the management of various collective goods and services in rural areas. According to Wade, people identify the statutory panchayat as an institution of the government and have very limited stake in it. They feel that the panchayat serves the interests of the individuals who control it, that the panchayat is concerned only with government-approved work and that, on the contrary, the local traditional council is concerned with the betterment of the village. This is a sharp distinction perceived by the people between the village panchayat and the traditional local council. Wade's study shows that the local councils of the people function independently of the legally established panchahati raj system. Many of the resources which technically belong to the village panchayat and other departments of the state are practically used by the people under the coordination of the local council and such arrangements are found to be stable and efficient.

In their study of the management and use of common property resources in Tamil Nadu, India, Blaikie, Haris and Pain found that the common property resources in villages are not maintained properly by the village panchayats.[8] In the name of the village panchayat, these resources are exploited by individuals who are powerful and have contacts with the government officials associated with the panchayati raj system. Even though local traditional village councils do exist, they are not able to protect the common property resources from such exploitation by individuals.

Nirmal Sengupta, in his study of the management of common property resources in Andhra Pradesh and Tamil Nadu, points out that, in many places, the village panchayats are not able to mobilise the people for the maintenance of resources like irrigation systems, whereas the traditional local institutions are able to organise the people for that purpose.[9]

Sasikant, in his study of the management of common property resources in the Binj Giri Hills of Orissa, avers that the local communities are in a better position to mobilise people for the upkeep of common property resources than the statutory village panchayats.[10] The reason offered by him is that, in Orissa, while the village panchayats have been established to cover a large number of hamlets, the local community systems remain intact, actively fulfilling the needs of the community. These communities are homogeneous in nature and have been traditionally involved in the protection and management of water bodies, community lands and village temples.

Blair, who has done extensive research on common property resources management in India and Nepal, has stated that the panchayats are not successful in managing common property resoruces with people's participation.[11] The panchayats look at these resources as income generators for panchayat programmes and not as community assets of the villages to meet the people's needs. Most panchayats prefer to auction the benefits of such assets to outsiders who can pay the best price rather than use them for the crucial needs of the local people. Wood lots, fisheries and fruit bearing trees are some of the resources of the villages often auctioned by the panchayats to outsiders. Blair feels that, in small homogeneous and cohesive groups, it is easier for the cultural norms of a moral economy to complement the purely rational economic calculus of methodological individualism. Based on the above views, Blair argues that local users' groups fare much better with common property resources because they can restrict membership and thus avoid free riders and because they can establish close relationship in the members' mind between the benefits and the costs of participating in a group discipline to maintain the resource.[12]

Vani, in her study 'Role of Panchayat Institutions in Irrigation Management', has explained many structural problems involved in ensuring people's participation in the panchayats' efforts for the management of irrigation tanks. She argues that, unless effective structural changes are introduced in the panchayats, people's participation will be a distant dream in the management of irrigation tanks. At the same time, she finds that, in some villages of Chengalpattu district of Tamil Nadu, the local communities clear channels every year, undertake repair work, and, keep watch on the bunds reglarly, and that these functions have not been recognised by the panchayats.[13]

When people are ready to do such work, the panchayats are not able to use the participatory spirit of the people for the management of irrigation tanks and other natural resources.

There is no significant study available in this direction relevant to Tamil Nadu to find out why people constitute local organisations to attend to functions relating to panchayats. This study tries to fill this existing gap in the body of knowledge in this area.

Theoretical Perspective

A considerable quantum of knowledge is available to explain the participation of people in development programmes and processes related to common assets affecting them collectively in rural areas. Some of the natural resources like irrigation tanks, grazing lands, forests and other common assets are being jointly used for generations and are crucial to the life of the rural people. Even though most of these resources are owned by various departments of the state, in practice, and by tradition, local management systems do exist for the management of these resources. Panchayati raj institutions are given the responsibility of the management of some of the local resources in rural areas like irrigation tanks, village ponds, unreserved forests, grazing lands, waste lands, threshing grounds and fisheries. In managing these resources the panchayati raj institutions are given the responsibility of facilitating people's participation. Despite the professed faith of most of the development planners in people's participation in the development process, it is, by and large, still a distant dream.

There are cases of collective management of common assets by people for many years without much state support. There are also cases of neglect of crucial collective assets because of lack of interest on the part of the local people in spite of state support through various development programmes. This has been explained by many researchers, and a variety of theories have been developed on this subject over the years.

Hardin's Theory of Tragedy of Commons

Hardin's Theory of Tragedy of Commons is classified as collective action pessimist theory. Hardin, in his article published in *Science* (1968), argues that individuals as self seekers are not capable of managing common assets collectively among themselves. He characterises this characteristic as 'the tragedy of commons'. Hardin illustrates the logic of the tragedy of commons by a parable.[14]

Hardin asks the reader to envision a "pasture open to all". He examines the structure of this situation from the perspective of a rational herder. Each herder receives direct benefit from his own animals and suffers delayed costs from the deterioration of the commons when his and others' cattle over-graze. Each herder is motivated to add more and more animals because he receives direct benefit from his own animals and bears only a share of the costs resulting from over-grazing. Each herder is locked into a system that compels him to increase his herd without limit. Ruin is the destination towards which all the individuals rush, each pursuing his own interest in a society that believes in the freedom of the commons.[15]

Hardin argues that individuals are bound to be self seekers as they are not assured of the behaviour of other individuals in using a common asset collectively. Each rational user of a common asset or resource is motivated to consume or use the resource more and more till the resource or asset is degraded as a result of uncoordinated use by all the individuals in the community. Thus individual rationality leads to collective irrationality.[16] Every individual tries to obtain maximum benefit at the cost of the other individuals or at the cost of the public.

Hardin's theory is basically pessimistic about voluntary collective action by individuals for collective good. The policy implications of Hardin's theory are far reaching. It has become a dominant paradigm of the management of common assets. Hardin's theory is used for justification of state intervention in the management of common resources.[17] It is also used to justify the large scale privatisation of resources. The right of the people who have used some of the resources like irrigation systems, forests and fisheries for centuries are taken over by the state authorities in many parts of the developing countries. Hardin's theory helps scholars explain the large scale degradation of crucial natural resources and the failure of the people to effectively participate in the management of these resources.[18]

But, the logic of Hardin's theory is not acceptable to many scholars like Ostrom,[19] McKean,[20] Runge[21] and Wade.[22] They give empirical evidence to prove that collective action for the management of common resources is widely in practice all over the world, contrary to Hardin's assumption. One criticism against Hardin is that the theory of the tragedy of commons regards all resources used collectively as 'open access resources' (resources used by unrestricted number of individuals and open to any one to use without any conditions or restrictions). But, traditionally, many resources have been used by specific groups collectively under certain regulations prescribed by the authorised users of the resources. Such management systems sometimes have legal sanction also. So, Hardin's theory is not found adequate to explain different systems of management of common resources collectively by individuals. Attempts have been made by scholars to identify certain conditions under which individuals will seek collective good by their joint efforts.

The Game Theory of Prisoner's Dilemma

Hardin's theory is supported by the Game Theory of Prisoner's Dilemma. It is also explained by a parable.[23] Two accomplices to a murder are arrested by the police and kept separately, without any chance for communication. Each of them is assured that he can defect against the other by confessing, for which he will be granted acquittal. But, if both of them confess and their confessions are not so valuable, instead of the death sentence, they may get a lesser punishment. If both refuse to indict the other, they cannot be convicted because of absence of sufficient evidence in such a situation. What can prisoners to do? If they are rational, one must confess to indict the other. Whatever be the strategy selected by the other, the confessor gets the better result by using this option, because, if the other person does not also confess, he gets acquittal by defecting. If his accomplice also defects, he still avoids the death sentence by defecting and escapes with a lesser punishment. In the end both of them find that they have got a lesser punishment by choosing their individual benefit, but in the process, have sacrificed a still better choice of acquittal achievable only through mutual cooperation and assurance. In this situation individuals have to suffer by not cooperating with each other for the collective good. Wade argues, "Prisoner's Dilemma has exercised a continuing fascination on social theorists because it appears to provide a solid basis for a profoundly disturbing conclusion, that rational people cannot achieve rational collective outcomes. It seems to be applicable to all situations in which it is possible for some to refuse to cooperate while others are willing to cooperate."[24] Wade maintains that, if the individuals have a chance to communicate with each other freely, and, if they are able to repeat the game again and again, they will learn to cooperate to get the maximum rational profit out of the game. Wade explains the situations in which individuals can cooperate for collective good. Free riding or defection remains a possibility but not an imperative in the Game Theory of Prisoner's Dilemma.[25]

The problem here is assurance—assurance regarding the behaviour of the other individuals. Institutions which give people the assurance that, if they follow the rules, they will not be the losers and that those who do not comply with the rules will be punished, greatly enhance the chance of voluntary compliance.[26] Rules have to be observed voluntarily because the cost of the enforcement of rules by the state when a large number of people have to be persuaded to comply involuntarily is likely to be prohibitively high.

The management of common resources should be modelled as a recurring game in which the chance for undetected defection is very difficult and the participants have reasonable control over the situation. The theory of Prisoner's Dilemma helps one to understand the behaviour of individuals when they work collectively for a common good.

Olson's Theory of Collective Action

There is another theory developed by Olson which explains collective action. Olson's Theory of Collective Action helps to understand the difficulties of individuals in cooperating to deliver collective good. Olson explains under what conditions individuals can provide themselves with collective good without relying on coercion or any positive inducement apart from the collective good itself. She argues :

> Unless the number of individuals in a group is quite small, or unless there is coercion or some other special device to make individuals act in their common interest, rational, self interested individuals will not act to achieve their common or group interests.[27]

According to Olson, free riding (on the back of those who voluntarily contribute) is possible in large groups in general. The larger the group, the less noticeable the actions of its individual members, the higher the transaction cost of bringing them together, and, hence, the higher the tendency for free riding. This is why large groups find it very difficult to provide collective good for their members.[28] Olson classifies groups into small, large and intermediate, depending on the size of the group. A small group is one in which a single individual has an interest in providing public good irrespective of the contribution of the others. "This is because in some small groups each of the members, or at least a few of them, will find that his personal gain from having the collective good exceeds the total cost of providing the collective good."[29]

Olson does not specify the number of individuals that would make a small group, but he argues that the group should be small enough so that the individual actions of any one or more members are noticeable to any other individual of the group.[30] Intermediate and large groups are those where no one individual has this interest and where some cooperation is therefore necessary. Olson argues that the likelihood of voluntary collective action (without selective punishments or inducements) is high for small groups, low for large ones and indetermediate for intermediate groups.[31]

Later, Olson also explains the role of the political entrepreneur in promoting collective action: "A political entrepreneur is an individual with a combination of such traits as leadership, the trust of the community or its fear, the ability to discern the motivations of others, and the desire to organise the group for collective action."[32] The success of the political entrepreneur is positively related to his ability to use selective incentives to motivate participation in collective action. Possibly, the presence of a such a person provides the required assurance to the members for participation.

Olson's theory helps to explain the relationship between voluntary participation and factors like the size of the group, the nature of benefits to the participants, and the presence of the political entrepreneur.

Property Approach to Common Property Resources Management

(i) State property resources, where the secure claim rests with the government—as in a government forest or a national park;

(ii) Private property resources, where the claim rests with the individual or the corporation; and

(iii) Common property resources, where the individuals have claims on collective goods as members of recognised groups.

In addition, resources may exist wherein there are no clear and secure claims and therefore cannot be considered property as classified above. Access to such a resource is available to everyone, making it the property of no one. It is generally classified as open access resource. Common property resources are a special class of property wherein individuals have rights and access to resources over which they have collective claims. Common property is created when members of a group agree to limit their individual claims on resources in the expectation that the other members of the group will do likewise. If individuals contribute to collective resources management without expecting others to contribute, they are behaving altruistically. If individuals do not contribute to the management of collective resources but expect all the others to contribute, they are behaving as free riders. Free riders wish to ride on the back of the other contributors, without contributing to the collective good. Altruism cannot be depended upon to sustain common property resources. Free riding, if uncontrolled, will be the basis of the tragedy of commons, as enunciated by Hardin.

Problem of Assurance and Institutional Solution

The writings of Wade emphasise the need for assurance to liberate individuals from the problem of prisoner's dilemma. As Hardin's theory says, each man is locked into a system that compels him to increase his self interest without limit. Assurance is the key to solve the problem of destructive self interest. Wade says, "Institutions which give people the assurance that if they do comply with the rules they will not be the sucker—that those others who do not comply will be punished—greatly increase the chances of voluntary compliance."[34]

Wade argues that it is very important because the law, as a mechanical barrier—whether local law or national law—can be effective when only a tiny minority of the population is likely to break it. He says that most observance of rules to be voluntary because the cost of enforcement when a large number of people comply involuntarily (through calculus of evasion and punishment) is likely to be prohibitively high.

Wade argues that, in a village situation, common resources use does not attract the assumptions of the prisoner's dilemma theory, because resource use is a recurring game in which the possibility of undetected free riding is fairly low, particularly in villages which have some structure to regulate the resource use.[35] Here the importance of local institutions is a determining factor which can help avoid the tragedy of commons by giving assurance to the individuals and liberating them from the trap of "compelling unlimited self interest". Individuals are assured that their contribution to the collective good will be suitably rewarded by the efficiency of the institution which regulates the behaviour of every individual.

In the context of natural resources management, Ostrom enunciates certain principles on which local institutions can function as long enduring self governing institutions. After empirical studies in many parts of the world on self governing institutions engaged in management of natural resources, Ostrom suggests certain conditions on which individuals, through institutions, could work towards collective management of natural resources. Ostrom calls them design principles for long enduring self governing systems. Ostrom has applied these principles in studying participatory institutions engaged in management of irrigation and other natural resources.

Ostrom's Design Principles for Long Enduring Self-governing Systems

Ostrom, after a number of empirical studies on collective action for the management of common property irrigation systems, found certain principles which are the key determinants of the participation of individuals in the management of common property resources.[36]

(i) Boundaries of the resource and the membership of the users of the resource are to be clearly defined.
(ii) The proportional equivalence between the benefits and costs must be maintained among the members of the users' group.
(iii) The members of the users' group must have a role in making and modifying the rules of the management of the resources. Most individuals affected by the operational rules are to be included in the group that modifies these rules.
(iv) The users must have control over the persons who monitor the physical condition and the behaviour of the users or the users themselves must monitor.
(v) The violator of the rules must receive graduated sanctions (depending on the seriousness and context of the offence) from other users, from officials accountable to users or both.
(vi) Users and their officials must have rapid access to low cost arenas to resolve conflict between users or between users and officials.
(vii) Rights of the users to devise their own institutions are not to be challenged by external governmental authorities.
(viii) Appropriation, provision, monitoring, enforcement, conflict

resolution and governance activities are to be organised in multiple layers of nested enterprises.

Ostrom's principles help to explain the impact of restricted membership, the use of the resource under restrictions, users' control over rule formulation and rule enforcement, sanctions for violation of rules and conflict resolution by users themselves, and, users' right to shape the institutions governing the resources. Ostrom also explains the importance of various activities being organised in multiple layers of nested enterprises. Ostrom's principles help in understanding the problems related to the collective management of common property resources in general and irrigation systems in particular. According to her, a community of members sharing a common culture, knowledge of the resource and knowledge of the resource use, facilitated by simple rules and regulated by self-governing organisations are capable of ensuring of common good by collective action.

Methodology

Based on the theories discussed above the objectives and hypotheses of the study have been set as hereunder :

Objectives

The objectives of the present study are :

(i) To study people's perception of the assurance provided to the people by local community organisations and panchayats in the management of panchayat irrigation tanks.

(ii) To study people's perception of participation facilitated by local community organisations and panchayats in the management of panchayat irrigation tanks.

Hypothesis

The study has the following two hypothesis :

1. In the perception of the people, local community organisations provide better assurance to the people than panchayats in the management of panchayat irrigation tanks.
2. In the perception of the people, local community organisations facilitate greater participation of the people than the panchayats in the management of panchayat irrigation tanks.

Variables Used in the Study

This study primarily focuses on the effect of organisational arrangements on people's participation in the management of irrigation tanks. In the first hypothesis assurance is regarded as a dependent variable and institutional arrangements are regarded as independent variables. In the second hypothesis people's participation is taken as a dependent variable and institutional arrangements are regarded as independent variables.

Indicators Used in the Study to Evaluate Participation[37]

1. Participation in meetings
2. Participation in the decision-making process
3. Participation in maintenance of irrigation tanks
4. Participation in the repair of tanks in emergencies
5. Participation in distribution of water
6. Participation in managing water scarcity
7. Participation in conservation of trees
8. Participation in grazing regulations
9. Participation in conservation and community sharing of fisheries in the tank.

Indicators Used in the Study to Evaluate Assurance[38]

1. Protection of the interests of the people
2. Maintenance of boundary
3. People's control over the organisation

4. Stability of the organisation
5. Equity provided by the organisation
6. Autonomous status of the organisation
7. Adaptability of the organisation
8. Efficiency of the organisation
9. Sustainability of the resources
10. Accountability and Transparency of the organisation.

Tools and Techniques

To test the hypothesis of the study two sets of indicators to measure the two dependent variables, namely assurance and participation, have been developed.

While using the tools and techniques of data collection, the model used by Jodha for his well-known study of common property resources has been consulted.[39] Jodha has used a variety of techniques and tools for data collection. They are records of oral histories, physical verification of status of natural resources, participatory observation, group discussions and study of case histories. He believes that structured surveys have only limited value and are not sufficient to study complex issues relating to community participation in the management of common resources.

In this study the following tools and techniques were used. They were group discussions with village panchayat Presidents of Kalayarkovil Panchayat Union, interviews with panchayat union councillors, group discussions with the members of Local Community Organisations (LCOs), group discussions with Scheduled Caste (SC) people, group discussions with the development workers of a local non-government agency, participation in LCO meetings, discussions with revenue and panchayat officials, and, discussions with the workers of the LCOs and discussions with opinion makers in the villages. The relevant records available in the village panchayat, the panchayat union, the revenue officer and the LCO were studied.

A structured schedule was prepared to collect data on the perception of the households in the villages. The heads of the households were interviewed. In his or her absence any available member of the household was interviewed. A separate schedule was prepared for the village panchayat Presidents and interviews were conducted.

The data collected for the study, as per the suggestion of Jodha, were analysed by a simple method involving bivariate tables. Jodha argues that the relative simplicity and transparency associated with this method of data processing is very useful for understanding the problems and that it is very useful for designing development programmes. The hypotheses of the study were tested against the background of the theories discussed earlier and the available data.

Participatory observation and physical verification were very useful for this study. The researcher observed the village assembly meetings and Gram Sabha meetings. The researcher also observed the distribution of water and scarcity management and people's involvement in them. The researcher could personally see the effects of participatory resources management over several decades in the ecological development of the study villages. The supply channels and field channels were physically verified. The condition of the trees in the village commons and in private lands was physically checked.

Operational Definitions

The key concepts used in the study are operationally defined hereunder.

1. Panchayats

Panchayats are the rural local governments established by the Tamil Nadu Panchayat Act, 1994 to facilitate people's participation in development programmes at the grassroot level. For this study the village panchayats and the panchayat unions are taken as panchayats.

2. Local Community Organisation

The Local Community Organisation is an organisation locally evolved by the people in the study villages to work collectively to achive their common felt needs. They are involved in a variety of functions in villages including the maintenance of irrigation tanks. These organisations do not have any legal status as per the accepted parlance of the government. Yet, they have social saction.

3. Participation

For this study participation is defined as the process wherein people contribute to the attainment of institutions' objectives, share the benefits from common activities, and, follow rules, regulations and other decisions made by the institutions in the context of management of irrigation tanks and related natural resources.

4. Assurance

For this study assurance is defined as the guarantee given by the institution to the people that the prescribed rules of the institution will be followed by all concerned and that the interests of the contributors will be safeguarded. Moreover the resources will be sustained and the institution is sufficiently autonomous, stable and efficient to discharge the above mentioned responsibilities and maintain equity in its dealings with the participants.

5. Irrigation Tanks

An irrigation tank is a small reservoir constructed across the slope of a valley to harvest and store rain water during rainy seasons to be used for irrigation during dry seasons. For this study rainfed irrigation tanks with less than 100 acres of command area, which are entrusted by the state to the panchayats as per the Panchayat Act, have been taken.

6. Natural Resources

The term covers irrigation tanks, water shed of the irrigation tanks, forestry and fishery of the irrigation tanks and common lands organically linked with the irrigation tanks in the study area.

Selection of Study Area

For this study two villages from Sivagangai district were selected for the following reasons. Sivagangai and Ramnad are two districts of Tamil Nadu which have more than 80 per cent of the total irrigated area under tank irrigation. Between the two districts Sivagangai has the larger number of irrigation tanks. The district depends mainly on rainfed tank irrigation for its agriculture and it is industrially backward. Wade argues that, in such a situation, the chance for people's participation in the collective management of resources is high because of the problems of scarcity and risk.[40] A study by Sengupta in Sivagangai district also indicates the prevalence of community participation in tank management.[41] A study by Gandhigram Rural Institute in Kalayarkovil Block indicates that a number of LCOs are functioning there with focus on tank management and with active people's participation and the study identifies twelve villages.[42] Out of these twelve, two villages were selected for the present study by lottery method.

Sampling

For this study two villages located in two village panchayats of Kalayarkoil Panchayat Union in Sivagangai district are selected. The first village selected for the study is Pulikanmai located in Paruthikanmai village panchayat. In this village a LCO is functioning. There are 161 households in the village as per the records of the LCO. Out of this 41 are SC households and 120 are backward class households. Twenty-five per cent of the households have been selected for the study by random sampling method with due weightage to SC households. Out of 40 households selected for the study, 10 households are SC households.

The second village selected for the study is Periyakannanur. Periyakannanur is one of eleven hamlets located in Periyakannanur village panchayat. In this village a LCO is functioning. In Periyakannanur village there are 242 households as per the records of the LCO. Out of the 242 households 70 households are SC households. Twenty-five per cent of the households of the village have been selected for the study by random sampling method with due weightage to SC households. Out of the 6 households selected for the study 18 households are SC households.

Framework of Analaysis

The data collected by the structured schedules and other tools and techniques have been used to test the hypothesis in the light of the theoretical framework and the literature discussed earlier in this chapter. Jodha recommends the use of bivariate tables to analyse the data collected by the structured schedule for transparency, simplicity and applicability. Accordingly, the data collected have been classified in the form of tables and the same have been analysed and explained through descriptive analysis. In the discussions, the insights, experiences and perception of the people affected by the problem have also been used.

Delimitation

The study is limited to the participation of the people in the management of irrigation tanks from the perspective of the people. The study focuses on perception of the people who are critically dependent on irrigation tanks for their economic survival. The study concentrates on the facilitating role of the LCOs and the panchayats in people's participation in the management of irrigation tanks. The study does not cover other social and economic issues of the study area like land distribution or gender and caste discrimination in detail.

Limitations of the Study

Generally LCOs are not ready to discuss their activities with any outsider. The LCOs fear that government officials may intervene in the working of their organisations. In spite of his repeated attempts, the researcher could not arrange any interactive exercise between the elected leaders and the officials of the panchayat departments and the members of the LCOs. Such a session could have elicited some valuable information on the interface between LCOs and panchayats.

Like many other institutions, the LCOs also have gender bias. The researcher was able to hold discussions with a number of women also. But equal weightage could not be given to women in the collection of data by the structured schedule.

One LCO (in Pulikanmai) maintains records meticulously. The other LCO (in Periyakannanur) does not maintain records properly. The panchayats do not maintain records properly. The panchayats are supposed to maintain a Kudimaramathu record. But Kudimaramathu records are not maintained. The record of community assets is not properly updated by the panchayats. The researcher faced some problems in verifying the records.

The researcher did not use any rigorous statistical methods in the study. After carefully studying the work of Jodha, the researcher had reservations about using such rigorous methods. Jodha has pointed out the limitations of such methods in studying issues of community management of natural resources.

Chapterisation

The study has five chapters. The first chapter introduces the study, states the problem taken up for study, reviews the available literature, furnishes the theoretical perspective, states the objectives and the hypotheses of the study, mentions the variables, the tools and the techniques used, provides operational definitions of key concepts used, describes the selection of the study, explains the sampling and the framework of analysis, specifies the de-limitation and the limitations of the study and spells out the chapterisation.

The second chapter provides background details about the question of participation.

The third chapter presents the profile of the study area and a descriptive analysis of the issues based on the data collected from participatory observation, oral histories, unstructured interviews, group discussions, physical verification of the resources and records.

The fourth chapter presents an analysis of the data collected by a structured interview with the respondents.

The fifth chapter presents the major findings of the study, suggestions for policy changes in the area of management of natural resources at village level and concluding remarks.

NOTES

1. Katar Singh, *Peoples Participation in Natural Resource Management*, Anand: Institute of Rural Management, 1992, p. 2.
2. Government of India, *The Constitution of India*, New Delhi, Article 40, 1996.
3. N.S. Jodha, "Rural Common Property Resources: A Growing Crisis", *Gate Keeper Series No. 24*, London: International Institute for Environment and Development, 1991, p. 10.
4. *Ibid.*
5. A.K. Gupta, "Why Poor do not Cooperate: Lessons from Modern Organisation", M. Clare, G. Wanger (Eds.) *Research Relationships Politics and Practice of Social Research*, London: G.C. George Allen and Unwin, 1987, pp. 117-127.
6. R. Brara, *Shifting Sands : A Study of Rights in Common Pastures*, Jaipur: Institute of Development Studies, 1987.
7. R. Wade, *Village Republic: Economic Conditions for Collective Action in South India*, Bombay: Orient Longman, 1987, pp. 30-31.
8. Piers Blaikie, John Harris and Adam Pain, "The Management and use of Common Property Resource in Tamil Nadu, India", Bromley W. Daniel, (Eds.) *Making the Commons Work : Theories and Practices*, Sanfrancisco: International Centre for Self-governance, 1992, pp. 253-254.
9. Nirmal Sen Gupta, *Managing Common Property: Irrigation in India and Philippines*, New Delhi: Sage Publications, 1991, p. 77.
10. Sasikanth, "Gandhian Approach to Management of Forest as a Common Property Resource: A Case Study of Binj Giri Hills in Orissa, India". *Paper presented in the First International Conference on Common Property Resources*, Durham: Duke University, 1990.
11. W. Harry Blair, "Democracy, Equity and Common Property Resource Management in Indian Sub-continent" in *Development and Change*, Vol. 27, 1996, pp. 475-499.
12. *Ibid.*
13. M.S. Vani, *Role of Panchayat Institutions in Irrigation Management*, New Delhi: The Indian Law Institute, 1992, p. 139.
14. G. Hardin, "The Tragedy of Commons", *Science* 162, 1968, pp. 1243-48.
15. *Ibid.*, p. 1244.
16. Katar Singh, *Management of Common Pool Resources—Principles and Cast*

Studies, New Delhi : Oxford University Press, 1994, p. 12.

17. Robert Chambers, N.C. Saxena, Tushar Shah, *To the Hands of the Poor Water and Trees*, New Delhi: Oxford and IBH Publishing Company Ltd., 1991, p. 163.
18. Katar Singh, 1994, *op.cit.*, p. 13.
19. E. Ostrom, *Governing the Commons: Evolution of Institutions for Collective Action*, New York: Cambridge University Press, 1990.
20. Cited in Katar Singh, 1994, *op.cit.*, p. 12.
21. Ford C. Runge, "Institutions and Free Ridder: The assurance problem in collective action", *The Journal of Politics*, 46, 1984, pp. 154-81.
22. R. Wade, *op.cit.*, p. 204.
23. Nirmal Sen Gupta, *Managing Common Property*, New Delhi: Sage Publication Pvt. Ltd., 1991, pp. 20-21
24. R. Wade, *op.cit.*, pp. 201-203.
25. *Ibid.*
26. *Ibid.*, p. 203.
27. M. Olson, *The Logic of Collective Action: Public Goods and the Theory of Groups*, Cambridge: Harward University Press, 1971, pp. 1-2.
28. Katar Singh, 1994, *op.cit.*, p. 32.
29. *Ibid.*, p. 34.
30. *Ibid.*
31. R. Wade, *op.cit.*, p. 206.
32. Katar Singh, *op.cit.*, p. 34.
33. J.N. Gibbs, Christopher and Bromely W. Daniel. "Institutional Arrangements for Management of Natural Resources: Common Property Regimes", Firket Berkes (Ed.), *Common Property Resources*, Dehradun: International Book Distributors, 1991, pp. 24-25.
34. R. Wade, *op.cit.*, p. 203.
35. *Ibid.*
36. E. Ostrom, *Crafting Institutions for Self-governing Institutions*, Sansfransisco: Institute for Contemporary Studies, 1992, pp. 62–79.
37. Indicators of participation is evolved by the researcher based on his field experience.
38. Indicators of Assurance used in this study have been adopted from the writings of Ostrom.
39. N.S. Jodha, "Studying Common Property Resources Biography of a Research Project", *Economic and Political Weekly*, March 18, 1995, p. 557.
40. R. Wade, *op.cit.*, pp. 183-187.
41. Nirmal Sen Gupta, *op.cit.*, p. 77.
42. V. Ragupathy, "A Survey on Kudi System in Sivagangai District Tamil Nadu", *Unpublished Report*, Gandhigram: Department of Political Science and Development Administration, Gandhigram Rural Institute, 1998.

2

TRADITION OF PARTICIPATION

Tradition of Participation in Tank Management

Tamil Nadu, a southern province of India, has more than 39,000 irrigation tanks.[1] These tanks are hundreds of years old. Most of the villages in Tamil Nadu are located near water bodies like irrigation tanks and ponds. In many areas, because of the climatic and topographical requirements, rain water has to be stored in tanks during rainy seasons. The system of storing water in tanks for irrigation has a tradition hundreds of years old.

"An irrigation tank is a small reservoir constructed across a slope of a valley to catch and store water during rainy season and use it for irrigation during dry season."[2] Traditionally, in the management of the tank, the local community was closely involved. The tank was normally treated as common property of the village.[3] The tank was used as a multipurpose resource to benefit almost the entire village community.[4] The tank in a dry region served as the main source of irrigation for agriculture. As rice is the major staple food of Tamil Nadu, paddy cultivation had great significance. The tank generated employment opportunity in the village and wages were paid in the form of paddy. The tank management and the responsibility of water distribution to the fields were normally with a section of the SC people and they got a share in the harvest.[5] People could get a variety of other benefits from the tanks and other common water bodies.[6] In some parts of Tamil Nadu, tank and pond water was used for drinking and other personal purposes. Particularly in areas like Ramnad and Sivagangai districts people took extra-ordinary interest in harvesting and storing the maximum rain water. Stored rain water was used by people in the dry seasons.[7]

The tank bed and the land adjacent to the tank were the main source of fuel and fodder for the village community. The tank area was a rich source for grazing. In summer the tank bed was used for cultivation of short duration crops like vegetables, greens, cucumber and cereals by the marginal sections of the village. The tank water was also used for fish culture. People had a good supply of fish for their use after the harvest season.[8] The tank bed was rich in fertile silt. Every year the silt was removed by farmers to be used as manure. Minor forest produce from the tank area was used by different sections of the society. Food materials, raw materials for different village crafts, building materials and medicines were collected from the tank area. The tank supported rich fauna and flora.[9]

In a self-sufficient rural economy the village was mostly dependent on the local resources for its survival and the significance of the tank in the village economy was very high. Without tanks many villages could not have existed in South Tamil Nadu. According to Sharma, "Human settlements are known to have disappeared along the ancient Mangamma Salai (Road) in Southern Tamil Nadu because tank seems to have been run out of water continuously for some years."[10] The tank provided food security to the village and functioned as the Green Bank of the village.

An illustrative list of the uses of the tank:

1. Water for irrigation
2. Water area for fish culture
3. Forestry in tank area
4. Fuel and fodder from tank area
5. Tank bed as a grazing area
6. Silt for farmers
7. Clay for pottery
8. Sand for construction
9. Land for cultivation in tank bed in dry season
10. Food material
11. Minor forest products

12. Timber for agricultural implements and buildings
13. Raw material for rural crafts
14. Water for bathing
15. Water for animals
16. Farm employment generation
17. Re-charging ground water
18. Habitat for flora and fauna.

The strength of the traditional system of management was the large number of people involved in the management of the tank.

Kudi System

Irrigation system and *kudi* system were interlinked in traditional Tamil society. The Tamil lexicon defines *kudi* as family, village, lineage and ryot family.[11] *Kudi* was a deep seated family in a village and was a member of the village community. *Kudis* were given certain duties and certain rights by the village community. Kudi covered not only farming families but also other serving families. *Kudis* were expected to participate in the maintenance of irrigation tank and other natural resources, which was called kudimaramathu. *Kudis* used to send representatives to the village assembly. Normally the seniormost male represented the *kudi* in the village assembly.

Village Assembly

Most of the villages in the Tamil country had village assemblies.[12] Every family or *kudi* in the village had representation in the village assembly. Participation of the SC families, however, was restricted. All other caste groups had representation. The village assembly had to meet regularly and attendance was obligatory. Discussions were held in open public meetings and decisions were taken only after transparent discussions. Accounts were submitted to the assembly and socially audited. The responsibility of implementing the decisions rested with the entire community. The village assemblies had to function mostly within the framework of well established traditions, customs and religious codes. Within the above said framework the village assembly enjoyed full freedom to take operational decisions. The village assembly had its own executive bodies. A scholar has identified seven types of executive committees.[13]

1. Committee of administration for the year
2. Committee for garden land
3. Committee for tanks
4. Committee for cultivable lands
5. Accounts Committee
6. Committee for roads
7. Committee of representatives of various bodies.

The Uthiramerur inscription of the Chola period gives details of the functioning of the village assembly.[14]

The strength of the system was the stability of the institutions and their capacity to mobilise the community in preserving and using the natural resources in a sustaining manner.[15]

Village Assembly and Tank Management

The major functions and powers of the village assemblies relating to the management of irrigation tanks are given hereunder.[16]

(a) *Construction of Tanks*
(b) *Maintenance of Tanks*

1. Annual maintenance work (kudimaramathu)
2. Desilting the tank bed
3. Maintenance of field channels
4. Preparation of irrigation calendar
5. Opening and closing of sluices
6. Strengthening of tank bunds
7. Removal of encroachments
8. Repair of sluices and surplus weir.

(c) *Raising Resources*

1. Fixing kudis' contributions in the form of labour, cash and in kind
2. Sale of water
3. Sale of land
4. Sale of fishing rights
5. Sale of grazing rights
6. Fines for violation of rules
7. Receiving gifts and endowments
8. Special cess for annual repair (Eriyam)
9. Leasing out of village common lands.

(d) *Management of Water Supply*

1. Deciding on cropping pattern depending on water availability
2. Drafting the irrigation calendar
3. Appointment of common irrigators
4. Appointment of watch and ward staff
5. Deciding on method of water distribution by duration and rotation
6. Deciding on sharing of water in times of scarcity
7. Imposing restrictions for economical use of water
8. Specifying certain fields to be irrigated from certain channels.

(e) *Settlement of Disputes*

1. Settlement of disputes over sharing, duration, frequency and rotation of watery supply
2. Controlling illegal use of water
3. Imposing fines and penalties for violation of rules
4. Framing rules for minimising disputes
5. Arbitration for resolving disputes
6. Using common irrigators and watch and ward staff to avoid disputes

7. Settlement of disputes over encroachment upon common lands
8. Field boundary disputes between individuals.

(f) *Emergency Functions*

1. Protection and repair of tank bunds, supply channel, sluices and surplus weir during floods.

(g) *Protection of Interests of Weaker Sections*

1. Granting land grants to serving castes
2. Fixing wages for common irrigators, field irrigators and watch and ward staff in the form of grain
3. Fixing share of the serving caste groups in the village in return for their services provided to the other families and ensuring proper payment
4. Fixing wages for agricultural labourers in the form of grain.

(h) *General Welfare*

1. Protection of natural resources
2. Regulation of grazing
3. Raising village common funds from the tank and other common resources
4. Regulation of collection and use of fuel, fodder and timber from the common land
5. Management of threshing grounds, cart stands, cattle grounds
6. Protection of fish in the water bodies and community harvesting of fish
7. Generation of village common fund
8. Contributions of funds, grains and labour for village temple and temple festivals
9. Protection of traditional rights of various groups
10. Protection of common resources from encroachment and unauthorised use.

Role of State

According to C. Moloney and K.V. Raju, the role of the royal government was supportive rather than proprietary. The local bodies were the proprietors, as evidenced hundreds of inscriptions. The local authorities possessed the required authority and skill for water management.[17] The state recognised the role of the village organisations and they were permitted to function as autonomous institutions. Above the village level, in many parts of Tamil Nadu, a federation of villages functioned with the name of Nadu. The administration of Nadu or country (federation of villeges) vested with the peasant representatives of the villages.[18] This body was responsible for collection of land revenue on behalf of the State. Scholars like Gomathinayagam argue that only the peasant leaders were responsible for the administration upto the level of the Nadu.[19] As many of the irrigation tanks had common watersheds there was a need for coordination of water management and the Nadu played a significant role in it. The representatives in the assembly of the Nadu were called Nattars.[20]

The Nattars were respected by the King, who consulted the Nattars in matters relating to their areas. The Nattars had not only administrative functions but also judicial functions. Disputes between villages were also brought before the Nattars for conflict resolution. But the main function of the Nattars was related to peasant issues and temple festivals.[21]

The traditional organisations were autonomous and free from state intervention. The organisations were evolved locally depending on the local responsibilities and after repeated experiments. Membership in the organisations was restricted to the families having a stake in the resources managed by the organisations.

Decline of Participation in the Management of Irrigation Tanks

Vani says, "However as a result of centralising force of colonialism, this indigenous and appropriate system of irrigation and village government, both met a similar and simultaneous fate — a slow and certain process of degradation."[22] The introduction of the *Ryotwari* land revenue system in the Madras Province in 1822 after the British conquest of the Tamil country was a landmark in the ecological history of Tamil Nadu.[23] Before that the Board of Revenue was established in the year 1786[24] and then the office of the District Collector was established in 1788 in the Presidency.[25] The District Collectors took over the land and other related resources and State ownership of common natural resources was established. Vani writes, "Under *Ryotwari* system many factors prevented united action by villagers, firstly the ryot contracted individually with the government to pay revenue on annual term and it was no longer a common arrangement with all ryots. Secondly under the terms of the tenure a ryot could keep or throw up his land, and take up new land relinquished by someone else. This practice would have eroded his sense of responsibility for the irrigation tanks and limited his interest to cooperating in the distribution of water. Thirdly all tanks and water sources except the private channels leading to fields vested in the government and it was recognised to be the government responsibility to see to the repairs and maintenance, and the ryots were only expected to contribute a share of the expense. Fourthly all waste lands in the village now belonged to the State and could not be used by villagers for any purpose. Fifthly the village headman and karnam were now government servants implementing company's regulations and much less oriented towards the village than formerly. Sixthly the high rate of assessments of land revenue left very little profit in the hands of the ryots which further discouraged the villagers from taking care of their irrigation works."[26]

The introduction of the Revenue Department and the judicial system eroded the rights of the local institutions over the management of natural resources and settlement of disputes at the village level.[27] The East India Company was interested in maximising land revenue and considered irrigation work a source of revenue. It ignored the need for village level institutional arrangements to facilitate popular involvement in maintaining irrigation tanks and other natural resources like forests, grazing lands and fisheries in the rural areas.[28] This policy of the State resulted in the neglect of these resources by people as these resources were considered state property and people's involvement was considered encroachment upon the authority of the

State. The decline of the irrigation system due to lack of popular interest in their maintenance and the new revenue system contributed to frequent famines in the first half of the 19th century.[29] During this period the East India Company experimented with the management of irrigation tanks. The civil engineers of the army were assigned the management of irrigation tanks.[30]

In the Madras Presidency an office of Superintendent of Tank Repairs was established in the year 1809 and civil engineers were entrusted with the task of tank management.[31] This office was upgraded as the Department of Tank Repairs in the year 1819.[32] In the year 1836 the Public Works Department was created and tank management was entrusted to it.[33] A centralised modern irrigation administration was established and irrigation was considered purely a technical matter and tanks were considered sources of revenue. "Government passed Madras Compulsory Labour Act in 1858 (or what was known as the Kudimaramathu Act) with a view to legalise compulsory labour for maintenance of tanks and repair in emergency by local community whenever breaches occurred due to inundations and also penalise non-performance of customary labour."[34] This Act forced the villagers to perform eight types of customary maintenance work by the joint labour of the village community in the tanks. The maintenance by the community was to be regulated by the village headman under the orders of Tehsildar. In case of any failure a fine could be imposed. But, even then, participation could not be enforced by the revenue officials. The Act forced the people to work for the maintenance of a government property over which people did not enjoy any property right.[35] All the attempts of the State to involve the people in the maintenance of tanks failed and the people were not ready to participate in tank management.

Panchayats and Irrigation Management : The British Experiments

The Madras Village Panchayat Act of 1920

The Madras Village Panchayat Act of 1920 was landmark in the history of local self-governance. The constitution of the village panchayat was voluntary and they were constituted only where there were requests from the villagers to form them. The Act provided scope for the constitution of many kinds of panchayats for forests, education etc. No particular function was obligatory. The village panchayats were free to select the functions included in the Act. Sections 18 and 19 of the Act were related to irrigation.[36] As per Section 18 of the Act, there was scope for transfer of the functions of any village irrigation work to the village panchayats.[37] Section 19 gave power to the village panchayats to act on the request of cultivators in the management of irrigation tanks even without a formal transfer of functions by the government.[38] Section 18 could transfer only the functions relating to irrigation and not the proprietorship of the water bodies. But the government rarely acted on this section and only two village panchayats in the Madras Presidency could benefit from this section even after six years of the enactment of the Act.[39] However, Section 19 of the Act was better used by the village panchayats. As per Section 19, even without any transfer of functions, the village panchayats, on the request of farmers, could organise Kudimaramathu. The Act gave powers to collect fees from farmers for Kudimaramathu work. According to Section 15 of the Madras Village Panchayat Act, the village panchayats were entitled to exercise control over cattle stands, threshing floors, topes and other communal porambokes.[40] Section 17 of the Act provided for the transfer of forests to the village panchayats. Even though there was scope for the village panchayats to manage common properties, the Departments of Revenue, Public Works, and Forests did not agree to the transfer of such resources. In most cases the District Collectors (inspectors of the village panchayats) did not permit such transfers. As Vani says, "The provisions of the Madras Village Panchayat Act, 1920 conferring powers over various resources on panchayats were merely conceptual. In reality, government holds the reins of control firmly in their hands."[41]

The Madras Local Board Act of 1930

Even though the Madras Local Board Act of 1930 provided for

Kudimaramathu and kaval (watch over crops) etc., the village panchayats did not have any means to raise funds to perform these functions. The Act was considered a setback to the involvement of the village panchayats in Kudimaramathu work and other works related to irrigation tanks. The government was not willing to give any financial powers or to transfer the natural resources to the village panchayats.[42]

Grow More Food Campaign 1946 and Kudimaramathu

As part of the 'grow more' campaign, Kudimaramathu of tanks was taken up at government expense. After three years of the campaign, the government felt that Kudimaramathu was to be taken over by the State gradually and that, if necessary, a separate cess could be collected from the farmers in lieu of their kudimaramathu liability.[43] The government gave the responsibility of tank maintenance work to the Chief Engineer for Irrigation of the Public Works Department in the year 1949 without any pretence at Kudimaramathu.[44]

The Kudimaramathu approach of the government failed because participation could not be forced by government orders. The British approach was technological and legal and it did not consider the human aspects of management. The resources were considered revenue generating sources for the government. The Madras Village Panchayat Act of 1920 and the Madras Local Board Act of 1930 provided for involving the people in resource management, but the reluctance of the State to part with the powers relating to these resources aborted the concept of participation.

Panchayats and Participation

Experiments in Democratic Decentralisation and People's Participation in Management of Irrigation Tanks and Other Natural Resources

The Constitution of India did not have any provision for democratic decentralisation and empowerment of the community with regard to natural resources. Scholars like P.J. Krishnan argue that the British approach of state ownership of natural resources was once again consolidated by the Indian Constitution. Krishnan says, "The Constitution of India as originally adopted was blind to conservation".[45] The Constitution makers did not visualise the need for restructuring the revenue administration and transferring resources to the local people. However, Article 40 of the Constitution, which is a directive principle of State policy and a non-enforceable article, says, "The State shall take steps to organise village panchayats and endow them with such powers and authority as may be necessary to enable them to function as units of self-government."[46]

Article 39(a), (b) and (c) says, "the State shall in particular direct its policy towards securing that citizens have the right to an adequate means of livelihood and that the ownership and control of the material resources of the community as best to subserve the common good that the operation of the economic system does not result in the concentration of wealth and means of production to the common detriment."[47]

Vani argues, "A review of land and water laws in the country in the light of the Article 39(a), (b) and (c) would reveal that they are inherently anti-panchayat and thereby violative of the Constitution. Land and water legislation that is now in force was enacted by a colonial government based on centralised administrative control. Whatever new legislation or amendments have been made, are made on that assumption."[48] However many states experimented with democratic decentralisation by enacting Panchayat Acts. The experiments in Tamil Nadu and their relevance to people's participation in natural resource management are discussed here.

The Government of Madras, to give effect to the directive principle of state policy, enacted the Madras Village Panchayat Act of 1950 in place of the Madras Village Panchayat Act of 1920. It came into force from 1st April 1951.[49] Even though the Act attempted to transfer functions relating to irrigation tanks to the village panchayats, this could not materialise. In the meantime, the Community Development Programme was launched and the focus on development programmes was shifted to the block level. The review of the working of the village panchayats and the development blocks by the Madras Government and the Balwantrai Mehta Committee resulted in the enactment of the Madras Panchayat Act of 1958.[50]

The Madras Panchayat Act of 1958

The Madras Panchayat Act of 1958 had the following structural pattern.

1. Village panchayats at village level
2. Panchayat union council at block level
3. District development council at district level.

The village panchayat was the base of the new structure and the panchayat union council was the focus of activities. The village panchayat Presidents constituted the panchayat union council and the council was practically controlled by the Presidents of the village panchayats. The panchayat union council had control over all development programmes taking place at the block level. The panchayat union Chairman, who was elected by the Presidents of the village panchayats, had control over the officials working at the block level. The first few years after the enactment of the Act of 1958, the panchayat unions and the village panchayat Presidents could actively involve themselves in the development programmes. Both these institutions were linked organically and the interests of the village panchayats were accommodated in the panchayat union council.[51] The district development council practically did not have any power and was under the control of the District Collector.

Irrigation Tanks and People's Participation in the Act of 1958

The Act of 1958 focused on the panchayat union council which was a federation or union of village panchayats. The panchayat unions were given powers in the areas of primary education, primary health, agriculture, animal husbandry, minor irrigation etc.[52] In the area of minor irrigation, Section 85 of the Act brought about significant changes. Section 85 of the Act said that the government could transfer the following functions to the village panchayat or the panchayat union.[53]

(i) Protection of irrigation works
(ii) Maintenance of irrigation works
(iii) Management of irrigation
(iv) Distribution and regulation of water supply.

Section 85 also says, "Village panchayat or panchayat union council shall have the power subject to such restrictions and control as may be prescribed, to execute kudimaramathu in respect of any irrigation source in the village and to levy such fee and on such basis for the purpose thereof as may be prescribed." The section does not relieve the local community from performing functions covered under the Compulsory Labour Act of 1858. The section also transfers the fishery rights, along with the irrigation work, subject to the terms and conditions as prescribed by the government.[54]

The transfer to the panchayats of duties relating to the irrigation tanks without sufficient powers was pointless. The panchayats were to execute the kudimaramathu or community labour, but the panchayats were not given power by the government to levy contributions for this purpose. Only the government could levy contributions. The fishery rights, transferred along with the irrigation work, were also subject to the terms and conditions prescribed by the government.

Under this Act, irrigation tanks with less than 100 irrigated acres were transferred to the panchayat union. The responsibility of protection, maintenance, management of turns of irrigation, and distribution of water were transferred to the panchayat unions at the block level. But the powers to permit the panchayats to undertake such functions were vested with the State Government. The Revenue and the Public Works Departments were still holding authority over the management of irrigation tanks and refused to permit the panchayats freedom of action.

The Panchayat Union Engineer was made very powerful, restricting the scope for people's participation at the local level.

Placing minor irrigation at the block level in strongly criticised by Vani: "It is fully indicative of the top down approach, dictated by the size of the budget and works to be done, by an agency completely alienated from the village community as a whole, or from village panchayat institutions. This approach has been instrumental in divorcing irrigation management from agriculture at village level. Nothing could be less conducive to the functioning of village panchayats as "Units of self-government".[55]

Poramboke Lands and the Act of 1958

The Act of 1958 gave scope for the transfer of six types of poramboke lands in the Ryotwari tracts to the village panchayats.[56] They were :

(i) Grazing lands
(ii) Threshing grounds
(iii) Graveyards and burning grounds
(iv) Cattle grounds
(v) Cart stands
(vi) Topes (groves).

These porambokes, entrusted to the panchayats, could be used as per the terms and conditions prescribed by the State. The village panchayats could regulate the use of these poramboke lands and collect fees for their use. The panchayats could use these lands to generate revenue for the village panchayats or for any other public purposes as per the prescribed terms and conditions.

The Act of 1958 was a bold initiative in the direction of democratic decentralisation.[57] However, the well established State was not ready to part with the powers vested with the Revenue Department over local natural resources. Only the functions were transferred but the ownership of the resources was retained with the State. As the inspector of panchayats, the District Collector regulated the use of the natural resources by the panchyats. The Act could not change the basic framework of 'state ownership of resources', which was well established by the British administration. In spite of its deficiencies, the 1958 Act encouraged the functioning of Panchayati Raj Institutions upto 1967. After that, gradually, the powers of the panchayats, particularly the panchayat unions, were eroded.[58] After 1986, elections were not conducted periodically. As a result, the panchayats were practically brought under the control of government officials.

Enactment of 73rd Constitutional Amendment Act and Tamil Nadu Panchayat Act of 1994

The 73rd Constitutional Amendment Act, passed in 1994 by the Indian Parliament, has made the panchayat a part of the Constitution. Periodical election once in five years, uniform three-tier system (at village level, intermediate level and district level), reservation for SC and Scheduled Tribe (ST), and, reservation for women are some of the significant features of the new system. The 73rd Constitutional Amendment Act regards Panchayati Raj Institutions as institutions of self-government. It has given authority to the legislatures of the State to enact laws for devolution of powers and functions to the panchayats to prepare plans for economic development and social justice and to implement schemes for economic development and social justice, including those in relation to matters listed in the Eleventh Schedule (Article 243-G). Out of the 29 items listed in Article 243-G, ten are directly related to natural resources management. They are :

1. Agriculture, including agricultural extension
2. Land improvement, implementation of land reforms, land consolidation and soil conservation
3. Minor irrigation, water management and watershed development
4. Animal husbandry, dairying and poultry
5. Fisheries
6. Social forestry and farm forestry
7. Minor forest produce
8. Drinking water
9. Fuel and fodder
10. Non-conventional energy sources.

Following the 73rd Constitutional Amendment Act, the Tamil Nadu legislature passed the Tamil Nadu Panchayat Act of 1994.

The Tamil Nadu Panchayat Act of 1994 has created the following three-tiers :

(i) Village Panchayat
(ii) Panchayat Union
(iii) District Panchayat.

A new institution, namely Gram Sabha, has been created, in which all eligible voters of the village panchayat are members. The Gram Sabha has to meet at least four times in a year. The Gram Sabha shall approve the village plan and the village budget and review the progress of the schemes entrusted to the village panchayat by the government. The village panchayat is constituted for a minimum of five hundred population and has a minimum of five members and a maximum of fifteen members in its council. The members of the village panchayat are directly elected by vote from the village panchayat wards. The President of the village panchayat is directly elected by the voters of the village panchayat area.

For each development block a panchayat union is formed. Contrary to the Act of 1958, in the new system, the panahcyat Presidents do not find membership in the panchayat union council. Members of the council are elected directly from the panchayat union wards for a minimum population of 5,000. The President and the Vice-President of the panchayat union are elected by the elected members of the panchayat union council from among themselves. The members of parliament and the members of legislative assembly elected from the panchayat union area are also ex-officio members of the panchayat union council.

For every district a district panchayat has been formed. The members of the district panchayat are elected from the district panchayat wards. The President of the district panchayat is elected by the members of the district panchayat.

A major deficiency of the Act is the absence of organic linkage between all the three-tiers.[59] In the Act of 1958, all the village panchayat Presidents were members of the panchayat union council.[60] Even though the panchayat union was provided with major powers including the management of irrigation tanks, it did not affect the interests of the village panchayats because the panchayat union was nothing but a federation of village panchayats and the panchayat union council a federation of village panchayat Presidents. But, in the new system, the panchayat union is completely free from the control of the village panchayats. Moreover, in the new system, the State Government has enormous powers to control the Panchayati Raj Institutions through the inspector of panchayats. Any resolution or decision of the panchayat can be suspended or cancelled by the inspector of panchayats.[61] The State Government has full control over the process of budget making. The decisions of the government's inspecting official on the budget are final.[62] The District Collector continues to have control over the village panchayats and the panchayat union council. The District Rural Development Agency, responsible for the implementation of rural development schemes, is headed by the District Collector.[63] The District Collector, the inspector of panchayats, and, the State Government have control over all the natural resources in the village.

The Tamil Nadu Panchayat Act of 1994 and Management of Natural Resources

The Tamil Nadu Panchayat Act of 1994 has continued all the major features of the Act of 1958 with reference to irrigation tanks and poramboke lands. Most of the rules made under the Act of 1958 also still continue.

Section 133 of the Tamil Nadu Panchayat Act of 1994 is given below :

Maintenance of Irrigation Works, Execution of Kudimaramathu

(1) Subject to such conditions and control as may be prescribed, the government may transfer to any village panchayat or to any panchayat union council the protection and maintenance of any irrigation work, the management of turns of irrigation, or the regulation of distribution of water from any irrigation work to the

fields depending on it.

(2) The village panchayat or the panchayat union council shall have power, subject to such restrictions and control as may be prescribed, to execute Kudimaramathu in respect of any irrigation source in the village and to levy such fee and on such basis for the purposes thereof as may be prescribed.

Provided that nothing contained in this section shall be deemed to relieve the village community or any of its members of its or his liability under the Madras Compulsory Labour Act of 1858 (Central Act 1 of 1858) in respect of any irrigation source in the village in case the village panchayat makes default in executing the kudimaramathu in respect of that irrigation source.

(3) Where the maintenance of any irrigation work is transferred under this section, the fishery rights of government in such work shall be transferred to and be vested in the village panchayat or the panchayat union council, as the case may be, subject to such terms and conditions including terms and conditions regarding the utilisation of the income, as may be specified by the Government.

Section 133 of the Act and the rules which are effective as on date are, in summary, as follows:[64]

(i) The Act has transferred only certain functions related to irrigation work to the panchayats.

(ii) The panchayat unions have been given functions related to irrigation tanks with less than 100 acres of irrigated land.

(iii) There is scope for transfer of irrigation works to village panchayats also in the Act. If any village panchayat makes a request for transfer, it can be considered within the provisions of the Act.

(iv) Along with irrigation tanks, the fishery rights also have been transferred.

(v) The transfer is subject to the terms and conditions prescribed by the State.

(vi) The panchayats and the panchayat unions have the duty of protection and maintenance of the irrigation works.

(vii) The panchayats may regulate the turn of irrigation or distribution of water.

(viii) The Revenue Department retains the power of appointing the water distributions.

(ix) The panchayat cannot determine the levy for Kudimaramathu and only the State can decide this.

(x) The levy can be collected only by the Revenue Department.

(xi) The panchayats can execute works related to tanks only through the Union Engineer, who is under the control of the Public Works Department (PWD).

(xii) Section 133 of the Act does not relieve the village community of the responsibility of attending to any emergency functions relating to breach of tank bund or any other physical structure during floods.

(xiii) Section 133 expects the village panchayat to attend to emergency functions relating to breach of tank bund or any other physical structure during floods.

(xiv) The District Collector may collect compensation from the panchayats for any damage that the panchayats may cause to any irrigation work or any part of it due to its malfeasance or misfeasance.

(xv) The maintenance work can be carried out only under the control of the Revenue Divisional Officer and the Public Works Department. The Public Works Department has technical control over the panchayats through the Union Engineer.

(xvi) The Government has the power to resume the functions relating to the transferred tanks without assigning any reason.

Management of Trees and Poramboke Lands

Trees in the panchayat union tanks are also vested with the panchayat union.[65] The panchayat union can plant trees in the tank bunds and tank bed. The income from the trees may be equally shared by the village panchayat and the panchayat union. The panchayat union may authorise the village panchayats to manage trees in the tank and to plant trees in the tank beds. The usufructs may be shared by them.

The village panchayat may plant trees in the tanks under the control of the PWD and the revenue may be shared between the village panchayat and the PWD. The usufructs may be enjoyed by the village panchayat.

The trees in the poramboke lands in the village panchayats may be managed by the village panchayats and the usufructs may be enjoyed by the village panchayats.

Water bodies with less than 10 acres of irrigated area are vested with the village panchayats and the trees in them may be managed and the usufructs may be enjoyed by the village panchayats.

Any unauthorised cutting of trees must be reported by the Village Administrative Officer to the Tehsildar with a copy to the Executive Officer of the village panchayat or the panchayat union. The Executive Officer of the panchayat must take appropriate legal action against the offender within thirty days and must send action taken report to the Tehsildar. In case of default on the part of the panchayat, the Tehsildar can take appropriate action in the concerned court.

Trees under Social Forestry Project

The Social Forestry Project was launched in the year 1981 with the assistance of the Swedish International Development Authority in 12,000 panchayats.[66] In almost all panchayat tanks trees were planted. The purpose was to ensure sustainable supply of fuel, fodder, small timber and other minor forest products to the local people. As per the project, after ten years of plantation, trees could be cut, and, twice in the next twenty years, trees could be re-harvested. The right to harvest and auction the trees under the project was with the Forest Department. Of the revenue, 60 per cent was to go to the panchayat union and 40 per cent to the Forest Department. Out of the 60 per cent share of the panchayat union, 20 per cent must be spent on regeneration of trees in the tanks by the panchayat union. The remaining 40 per cent was to be shared equally by the panchayat union and the village panchayats. But it is reported that even after several years of harvesting, many village panchayats are yet to get their 20 per cent share from the Social Forestry Scheme.[67]

Management of Fisheries

The District Collector has the power to sanction fishing rights on lease in respect of all the tanks in the district. The District Collector permits the village panchayats, the panchayat union and the PWD to lease the fishery rights in the tanks vested with them.[68]

The village panchayat may lease the tanks and other water bodies with it and the revenue goes to the village panchayat. The panchayat union may lease the tanks vested with it and the revenue goes to the panchayat union. The Fisheries Department may lease the tanks under the control of the PWD and the revenue goes to the State Government.

The panchayats may spend the revenue from fisheries on :

(i) Development of fisheries
(ii) Maintenance of irrigation sources
(iii) Development of food production.

In cases where the local community uses the fisheries available in their local area for the benefit of the local community, it may be regulated by the panchayats. In case of any misuse, the panchayat can ask for takeover of such resources after obtaining an order from the District Collector. In case there are fishermen's cooperative societies in the area, on their requrest, the panchayats have to give the water bodies to them on lease. The lease amount is determined according to the rules framed by the Government and the District Collector is empowered to change the lease amount. In case no fishermen's cooperative socity comes forward to take over the fishing rights, the panchayats may give them on lease to private individuals by public auction after getting permission from the District Collector. The panchayat may appeal against the orders of the District Collector (on matters relating to the fisheries) to the State Government.

Village Panchayat and Trees in Unreserved Forests

Section 120 of the Act of 1994 vests the unreserved forests with the village panchayats. Section 120 reads :

Transfer of Unreserved Forests to Village Panchayat

(1)(a) All unreserved forests in the village at the commencement of this Act shall vest in the village panchayat and be administered by it for the benefit of such village.

(b) In respect of every forest so vested, the village panchayat shall, if so required by the Collector, pay to the Government such rent as the Collector may, from time to time, subject to the control of the Commissioner of Land Administration, fix in this behalf.

(2)(a) If the Revenue Divisional Officer is of opinion that a village panchayat is not administering properly a forest vested in it under sub-section (1), he may by order, withdraw such forest from the control of the village panchayat for such period as may be specified in the order, not exceeding the period, if any prescribed in this behalf. He may in respect of such forest direct that it be vested in the panchayat union council and be administered by it.

(b) The Revenue Divisional Officer may, from time to time, by order, extend the period specified in any order issued under clause (a), subject to the period prescribed in this behalf.

(c) Before issuing an order under clause (a) or (b), a reasonable opportunity shall be given to the village panchayat to show cause against such issue.

(d) When an order is issued under clause (a) or (b), the village panchayat concerned may, within three months of the service of the order, appeal against it to the Collector and the Collector may confirm, modify or reverse the order.

(3) The Commissioner of Land Administration may, at any time, either *suo motu* or on application, call for and examine the record of any order issued by the Revenue Divisional Officer or the Collector under sub-section (2) for the

purpose of satisfying himself as to the legality or propriety of such order, and may pass such order in reference thereto as he thinks fit.

If, in the opinion of the Government, any unreserved forest vested in a village panchayat under Section 120 is required for any public purpose, they may, by notification, resume the possession and administration of such unreserved forest and, upon such resumption by the Government, all rights and interests created in or over such unreserved forest before such resumption shall, as against the Government, cease and determine.

As per the rules of the Government under the Act, the panchayats may take the following action :[69]

1. Panchayat may issue permits for grazing cattle
2. Goats may not be permitted to graze
3. Regulations on grazing may be imposed.

Village Panchayat and Use of Certain Porambokes in Ryotwari Tracts

Section 134, which gives powers to the village panchayats to regulate the use of certain porambokes, is given below :

Village Panchayat to Regulate the Use of Certain Porambokes in Ryotwari Tracts

1. The provisions of this section shall apply in ryotwari tracts.
2. The following porambokes, namely, grazing grounds, threshing floors, burning and burial grounds, cattle-stands, cart-stands and topes shall vest in the village panchayat, and the village panchayat shall have power, subject to such restrictions and control as may be prescribed to regulate the use of such porambokes, provided the porambokes are at the disposal of the Government.
3. The Collector, after consulting the village panchayat, may, by notification, exclude from the operation of this Act, any

poramboke referred to in sub-section (2), and may also modify or cancel the notification.

4. The village panchayat shall also have power, subject to such restrictions and control as may be prescribed, to regulate the use of any other poramboke which is at the disposal of the Government, if the village panchayat is authorised in that behalf by an order of the Government.
5. The village panchayat may, subject to such restrictions and control as may be prescribed, plant trees on any poramboke, the use of which is regulated by it under sub-section (2) or sub-section (4).

The panchayat may use the porambokes as per the terms and conditions prescribed by the State. It may impose any regulation on the use of the poramboke by the public including the regulation of grazing. The panchayat may prescribe fees for the use of poramboke lands. The poramboke lands under the panchayat are subject to the inspection of the revenue officials and the panchayat must permit such inspection.

A close study of the provisions of the Panchayat Acts and the rules under the Acts relating to the role of the panchayats reveals certain facts. The British revenue policy of state ownership of all natural resources still dominates the policy of the Government in free India. The right of the local people to manage and use the local resources has not been recognised. The Panchayat Acts of 1958 and 1994 have restricted the scope for people's participation in the management of natural resources. Kudimaramathu could not be carried out because of the above said factors. The Madras Compulsory Labour Act of 1858 is still considered effective and the local people are required to perform emergency functions at times of breach in the irrigation works without any power to manage the resources in normal times. The panchayats are expected to undertake certain functions relating to the natural resources. Most of them are not obligatory but only optional. The Panchayat Act has not transferred proprietorship or ownership of natural resources to the panchayats, but only functions and duties relating to certain resources. The Revenue, Forest, Fisheries and Public Works

Departments still have the power to control and regulate the functioning of the panchayats. The transferred resources can be taken back by the State at any time. Decisions of the panchayats can be reviewed by the State. In certain cases the panchayats must take prior permission from the State to take decisions. The State still regards these resources as sources of revenue and the importance of these resources in the day to day life of the rural people is not recognised. The transfer of tanks to the panchayat union has restricted the scope for people's participation at the village level. In the Act of 1958, the panchayat union was controlled by the village panchayats. In the Act of 1994 the village panchayats have no representation in the panchayat union. In this context people's participation cannot be ensured by the panchayats. As there is no village or hamlet level institution to mobilise people's participation in the management of these resources, the panchayats find it difficult to operationalise the concept of people's participation.[70]

Panchayat development is being attempted after Independence within the existing institutional framework of State monopoly over natural resources. In this context one cannot expect the panchayat institutions to play any effective role in irrigation. Panchayat and irrigation legislations, far from empowering these institutions in protecting, preserving and effectively utilising water resources, in fact actively discourage any activity beyond the limited role of distribution of water and contribution of free labour for repair and upkeep of works. Even this exists only on paper. In actual fact, farmers manage as best as they can, unaided by the government.[71]

The Panchayat Acts and the rules of the government do not consider watershed as an integral part of the village life. But M.S. Swaminathan calls a village a watershed community. The Act of 1994 does not have any scientific and integrated approach to resource management at the village level. Instead, four Government Departments have been permitted to work in a village watershed area without any coordination. This unscientific approach is a hurdle to effective people's participation at the village level. An experienced administrator, J.C. Pant, former Secretary, Rural Development, Government of India, points out the significance of hamlet level community organisations. He says 'there are communities living in hamlets which have an identity of interests on many matters particularly in matters of common property resources and natural resources.'[72] He can visualise the possibility of the management of common property resources by them on a sustainable basis. The successive Panchayat Acts did not seriously try to change the administrative structure of Land Revenue Policy introduced by the British colonial administration and to bring about effective community control over local natural resources. As the panchayats have to work within the existing revenue administrative framework, they find it difficult to work in the area of ecological development.

NOTES

1. K. Palanisamy, R. Balasubramanian, A. Mohamed Ali, *Present Status and Future Strategies of Tank Irrigation in Tamil Nadu,* Coimbatore: Tamil Nadu Agricultural University, 1997, p. 4.
2. *Ibid.*, p. 3.
3. Gomathinayagam, "Palanthamilar Pasana Perumai", *Dinamani Pongal Malar (Tamil)*, Madras, 1998, pp. 34-35.
4. *Ibid.*
5. Nirmal Sen Gupta, *Managing Common Property: Irrigation in India and Phillipines*, New Delhi: Sage Publications, 1991, p. 77.
6. Gomathinayagam, *op.cit.*, pp. 34-35.
7. *Ibid.*
8. Gnanaprakasam, "Vellai Veechu in Water Management", *Proceedings of National Seminar on Water Management*, Madras: Anna University, 1996, pp. 215-217.
9. K. Palanisamy, R. Balasubramanian, A. Mohamad Ali, *op.cit.*, p. 18.
10. Cited in *Ibid.*
11. University of Madras, *Tamil Lexicon*, Madras, 1982, p. 971.
12. Harichandran, *Panchayati Raj and Rural Development: A Study of Tamil Nadu*, New Delhi: Concept Publishing Company, 1983, p. 10.
13. *Ibid.*
14. State Planning Commission, *Report on Entrustment of Power to Panchayat, Madras: Government of Tamil Nadu*, 1998, p. 264.
15. Liela Narayanan, "Tank Management Change and Continuity, Rejuvenation and Extension of Traditional System", *Proceedings of National Seminar on Management of Irrigation Tanks*, Madras: Anna University, 1996, pp. 57-65.

16. State Planning Commission, *op.cit.*, pp. 262-264; C. Moloney and K.V. Raju, *Managing Irrigation Together*, New Delhi: Sage Publication, 1994, pp. 44-46; M.S. Vani, *Role of Panchayat Institutions in Irrigation Management*, New Delhi: The Indian Law Institute, 1992, pp. 18-21.
17. C. Moloney and K.V. Raju, *op.cit.*, pp. 44-46.
18. *Ibid.*
19. Gomathinayagam, *op.cit.*, p. 34.
20. *Ibid.*
21. *Ibid.*
22. M.S. Vani, *op.cit.*, p. 166.
23. S. Ramasamy, cited in A. Agarwal, S. Narayan, *Dying Wisdom*, New Delhi: Centre for Science and Environment, 1997, p. 250.
24. *Ibid.*, pp. 250-252.
25. M.S. Vani, *op.cit.*, p. 28.
26. *Ibid.*
27. Gomathinayagam, *op.cit.*, p. 34.
28. M.S. Vani, *op.cit.*, p. 30.
29. *Ibid.*
30. C. Moloney and Raju, K.V., *op.cit.*, pp. 44-46.
31. *Ibid.*
32. *Ibid.*
33. *Ibid.*
34. S. Janakarajan, "In Search of Tanks: Some Hidden Facts", *Working Paper* No. 97. Madras: Madras Institute of Development Studies, 1991, p. 3.
35. *Ibid.*
36. Government of Madras. *Madras Panchayat Act, 1920*, Sections 18 & 19.
37. *Ibid.*, Section 18.
38. *Ibid.*, Section 19.
39. M.S. Vani, *op.cit.*, pp. 73-74.
40. Government of Madras, 1920, *op.cit.*, Section 15.
41. M.S. Vani, *op.cit.*, p. 76.
42. *Ibid.*, pp. 76-77.
43. *Ibid.*
44. C. Moloney and K.V. Raju, *op.cit.*, p. 47.
45. P.J. Krishnan, "Legal and Policy Issues in Community based Conservation", A. Kothari, *et.al.*, (Eds.), *Communities and Conservation*, New Delhi: Sage Publication, 1998, p. 357.
46. Government of India, *The Constitution of India*, New Delhi, 1996, Article 40.
47. *Ibid.*, Article 39A.
48. M.S. Vani, *op.cit.*, p. 114.
49. Harichandran, *op.cit.*, p. 60.
50. V. Ragupathy, Panchayati Raj in Tamil Nadu, *One Step Forward and Two Steps Backward*, Gandhigram: PRA Unit, Gandhigram Rural University, pp. 2-3.

51. *Ibid.*, pp. 3-4.
52. *Ibid.*, pp. 3-5.
53. Government of Madras, *Madras Panchayat Act, 1958*, Section 85.
54. *Ibid.*
55. M.S. Vani, *op.cit.*, p. 123.
56. Government of Madras, 1958, *op.cit.*, Section 86.
57. V. Ragupathy, *op.cit.*, p. 2-3.
58. *Ibid.*
59. Department of Political Science, *From Participation to Self-Governance*, Gandhigram: Gandhigram Rural Institute, 1998, p. 3.
60. V. Ragupathy, *op.cit.*, p. 3-6.
61. *Ibid.*, p. 10.
62. *Ibid.*
63. G. Palanithurai, *New Panchayati Raj System at Work: An Evaluation*, New Delhi: Concept Publishing Company, 1999, p. 29.
64. Summary extracted from Tamil Nadu Panchayat Act, 1994 and the rules effective on it.
65. S. Pugalendhi, *Uratchigal, Peruratchigal, Uratchi Onriumgal Sattamum Nadaimuraiyum (Tamil)*, Madras: Poongodi Publishers, 1990, pp. 618-619.
66. K. Palanisamy, R. Balasubramanian and A. Mohamed Ali, *op.cit.*, pp. 43-46.
67. *Ibid.*, p. 46.
68. S. Pugalendhi, *op.cit.*, pp. 621-634.
69. *Ibid.*, pp. 562-563.
70. J.C. Pant, "National Policies for Natural Resource Management at Grassroot Level—Overview". *The Indian Journal of Public Administration*, Vol. XLIV, No. 2, April-June, New Delhi, 1998, p. 243.
71. M.S. Vani, *op.cit.*, p. 167.
72. J.C. Pant, *op.cit.*, p. 243.

3

INSTITUTIONAL ARRANGEMENTS AT THE GRASSROOT

Profile of the Study Area

Sivagangai is one of the twenty-nine districts of Tamil Nadu State located in the South-Eastern part of the State. Madurai is the nearest big city, located 43 kms away from the district headquarters, Sivagangai Town. It was formed in 1983 upon bifurcation of the erstwhile Ramnad district.

Administrative Divisions[1]

The district has been divided into two revenue divisions and six revenue taluks. It has two development divisions and 11 development blocks or panchayat unions, 437 village panchayats, 12 town panchayats, and 3 municipalities.

Population[2]

According to the 1991 census, the district has a population of 10,78,190.

Population Profile

Total population	10,78,190
Male	5,30,495
Female	5,47,695

Scheduled Caste population	1,73,369
Male	85,730
Female	87,639
Scheduled Tribe population	1,198
Male	608
Female	590

Ecological Features

The district has an area of 4,126.5 sq. kms.[3] The major part of the area of the district has sandy soil while a small portion has black soil.[4] The rainfall is erratic, the average rainfall being only 933 mm. The district receives most of its rainfall from the North-East monsoon, from August to November. The monsoon often sets in late, besides being irregular. The sandy soil land of the district does not retain water and moisture.

Because of the soil condition and the scarcity of rain, agriculture is mostly under tank irrigation. Out of the total geographical area of 4,04,526 hectares, the land area under cultivation is only 1,24,514 hectares.[5] It means that only 31 per cent of the land area is under cultivation. The major part of the land area (69 per cent) is not under cultivation because of the poor rainfall, the nature of the soil and the absence of irrigation facilities. Out of the 1,24,514 hectares under cultivation, 96,700 hectares are under irrigation of all kinds. Out of this 82,663 hectares are under tank irrigation. It means that nearly 66.33 per cent of the land under cultivation depends on irrigation tanks.[6]

Significance of Irrigation Tanks

Out of the total 96,700 hectares of land under irrigation 82,663 hectares are uner tank irrigation.[7] It means nearly 86 per cent of the irrigated area in the district is tank irrigated (The state average is 24 per cent). The district has 4,597 irrigation tanks. Out of this only 161 tanks are river fed and 4,436 are rainfed (96.4 per cent).[8] Out of the 4,597 irrigation tanks 4,025 are under panchayats and 572 are under the Public Works Department.[9]

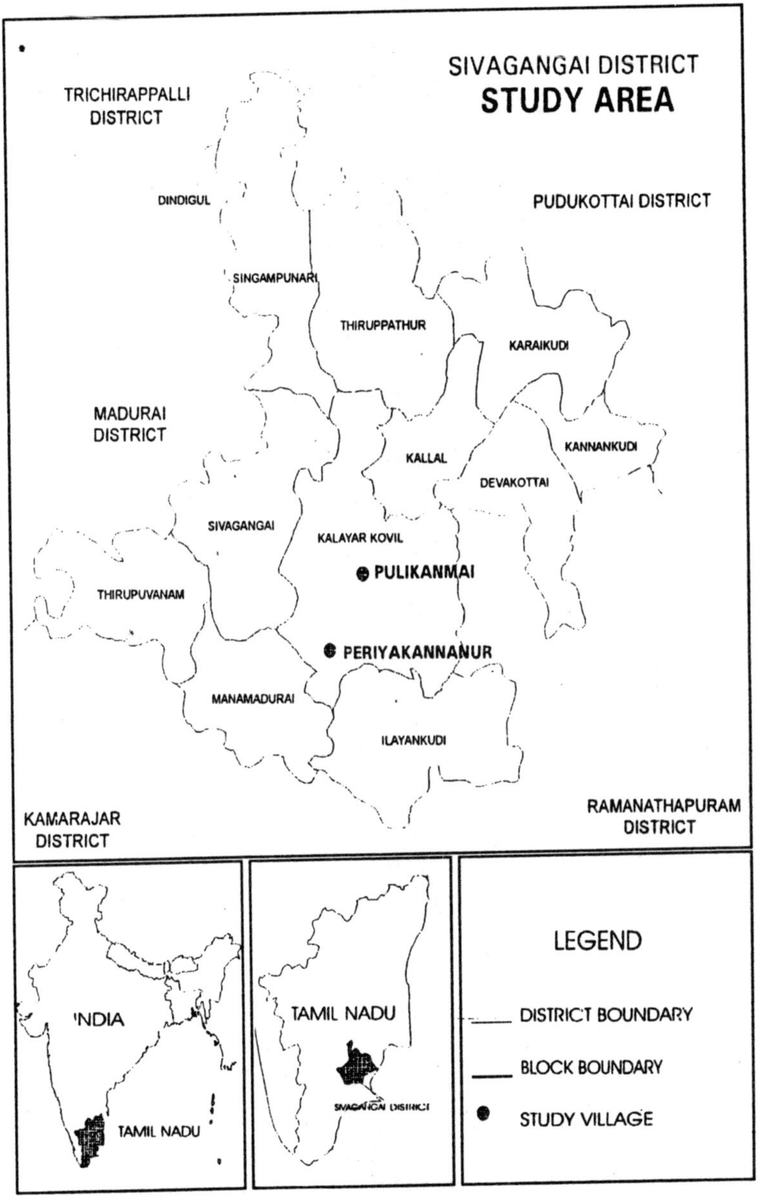

Map 3.1: Map of the Study Area

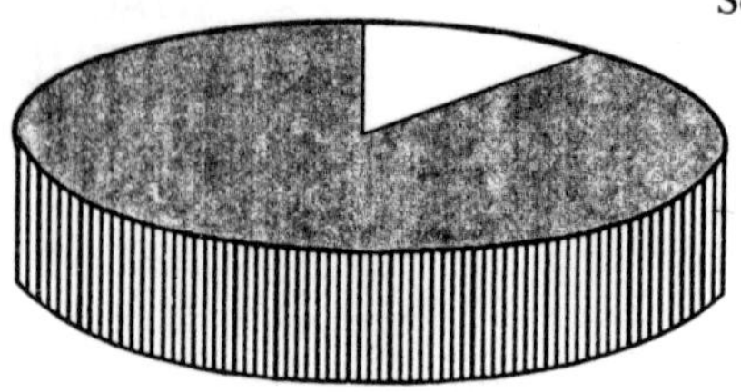

Fig. 3.1: Sivagangai District—Pattern of Irrigation

Source : K. Palanisamy, R. Balasubramanian and A. Mohamed Ali, *Present Status and Future Strategies of Tank Irrigation in Tamil Nadu*, Coimbatore: Tamil Nadu Agricultural University, 1997, p. 6.

Cropping Pattern

Paddy is the major crop in the district. Out of the total 1,24,514 hectares under cultivation, 80,482 hectares are under paddy cultivation.[10] It means 64.6 per cent of the land is under paddy cultivation. The next important crop is groundnut. In Sivagangai district, certain traditional varieties of paddy are cultivated as dry crop and semi-dry crop. The other crops in the rainfed land are ragi, maize and pulses. In recent years sugarcane has also been introduced in certain pockets where well irrigation is possible.[11]

Employment Status

Sivagangai is an industrially backward area. The scope for employment opportunity in industries is limited. There are a few textile mills in the district but most of them are sick units. As per the government records three-fourths of the working population depend on agriculture and only a small percentage of the people are employed in the organised industrial sector.[12]

Size of Landholding

As per the revenue records, 81 per cent of the farmers are small farmers holding less than 2.5 hectares of land. The details are given in Table 3.1.[13]

TABLE 3.1: Landholding Pattern in Sivagangai District

Sl.No.	*Size*	*No. of Holdings*	*Percentage*
1.	Below 1 hectare	2,55,212	80.9
2.	1.00 to 2.00 hectares	39,256	12.4
3.	2.01 to 4.00 hectares	16,077	5.1
4.	Over 4 hectares	5,080	1.6

Source : District Resource Profile, Sivagangai District 1997.

Table 3.1 shows that the landholding pattern in Sivagangai district is free from significance disparities. The pattern of land distribution provides a socio-economic setting conducive to building community based organisations in villages.

Cultural Ecology and Tradition of Rain Water Harvesting in the Study Area

The number of irrigation tanks in the village shows the significance of rain water harvesting in the district. For irrigation and drinking, rain water is harvested by the community. Almost in all villages, tanks, ponds, drinking water ponds and temple ponds are maintained. A scholar of cultural ecology, David Moose, who studied the irrigation tanks in Sivagangai district, regards the sandy type of soil, scanty rainfall and absence of alternative irrigation sources as the major contributors to the evolution of local institutions for the management of irrigation tanks in the district.[14] The areas of the district having light sandy soil are traditionally called *Mankala Nadu* or country with sandy soil.[15] The soil does not have water and moisture retention capacity. Rainfed farming is therefore not possible.[16] Hence storing rain water becomes a necessity. According to David Moose, the risk of tank breach is greater in the areas having light sandy soil.[17] During the rainy season tanks are to be watched carefully. Because of the soil condition frequent irrigation is required for the paddy fields. So there is a risk of water scarcity. Because of these reasons, institutionalising water management has become a part of the culture of the villages in this area.

Kalayarkovil Panchayat Union, where the study villages are located, is in the southern part of the district. It has a population of 94,718.[18] Out of the total population, 45,556 are males and 49,162 are females. There are 16,892 SC people in the union. Among them 8,243 are males and 8,649 are females. The panchayat union is classified as Grade III Panchayat Union because of its poor financial status.[19] The union has 43 village panchayats and one town panchayat. The panchayat union has 19 directly elected councillors, out of whom 11 are males and 8 are females. Among them there are two SC males and two SC females. The chairman of the panchayat union is a woman.

The panchayat union has 118 primary schools and 19 middle schools.[20] There are two high schools and eight higher secondary schools. The union has six primary health centres, one government maternity hospital and eight maternity sub-centres. The area is well connected by road with different parts of the district. The union has 118 km length of roads. The village panchayats maintain 97 km length of roads. There are 285 noon meal centres which benefit 16,508 children. There are 658 hand pumps and 58 electric pumps providing drinking water. The village panchayats maintain 3,239 street lights. The village panchayats have 256 radio sets and 320 television sets. In the union, as per the records, there are 30 women's clubs, with 750 members.

Cultural Ecology of Kalayarkovil Area

Kalayarkovil has a rich tradition of local self governance and collective management of common property resources. It has a temple of Lord Siva which is one thousand years old, with numerous inscriptions giving information on the village systems and natural resources in the area. The inscriptions give details of village committee, land use pattern, irrigation systems and land revenue system.[21]

Village assemblies and federation of villages were active for hundreds of years in this area. The federation of villages was called *Nadu* or Country.[22] The *Nadu* consisted of peasant leaders, who took decisions on areas of common interest like irrigation tanks, temple affairs, conflict resolution and management of juctice. Even at the time of the British rule the local systems were very active and maintained their independence.

The military records of the East India Company contain details of the local village institutions and their capacity to function autonomously.[23] The area was covered by thick forest and it was very difficult for the army of the East India Company to move about freely.[24]

The people of the area conserved the natural resources with great concern. The main sources of drinking water were the village ponds or *ooranis*. Ooranis were considered sacred properties of the village. Damaging the drinking water pond was considered a great sin. Construction of ponds was considered a respectable activity.[25] The irrigation system in the area was maintained by the LCO with great care. The village irrigation tanks were considered common properties of the village and everyone in the village benefited directly or indirectly from the tank. Recent studies in the area also give eivdence of the existence of strong community organisations and their interest in maintaining common property resources.[26] In view of these factors two villages in the panchayat union were selected for this study.

Community Maintenance of Drinking Water Ponds in the Study Area

Due to water scarcity and the salinity of the ground water in Sivagangai and Ramnad districts, local communities harvest rain water in open ponds. A few of these ponds are reserved only for drinking purpose. Strict community regulations in the use of these tanks are practised. Any violation of the rules prescribed would attract punishment. A drinking water pond was identified in a village

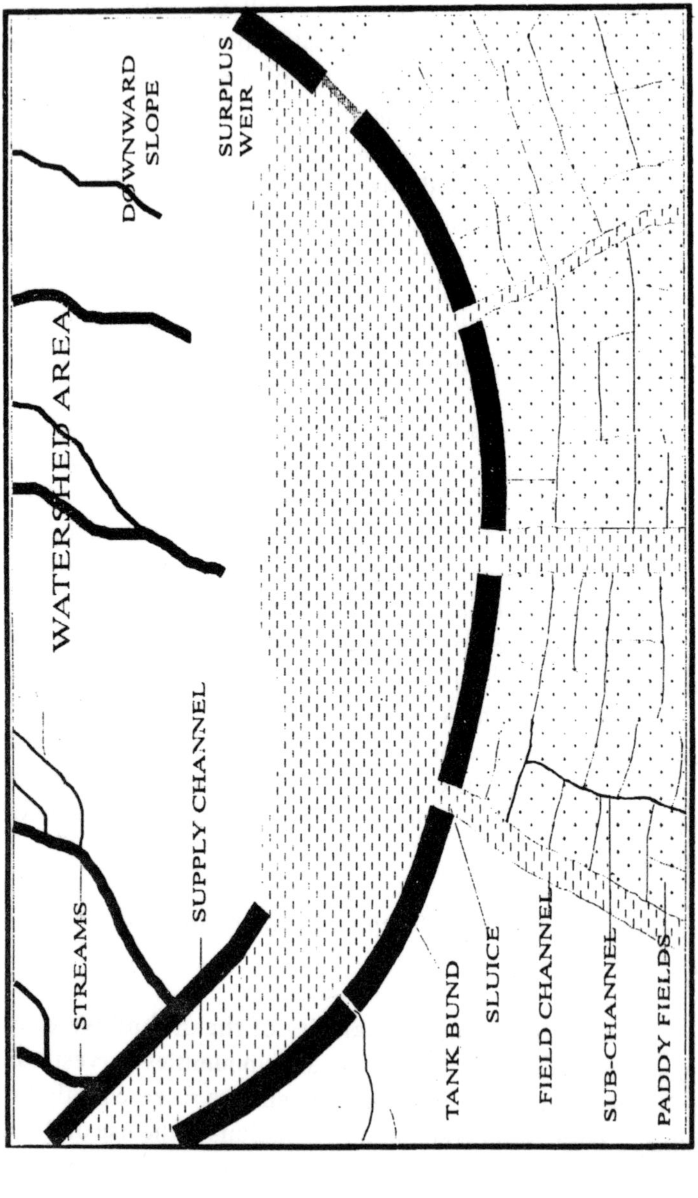

Fig. 3.2: Components of an Irrigation Tank

in the study area.[27] Because of the efforts of the LCO the pond was desilted and deepened by voluntary labour contribution by the villagers. Around 500 man days, worth about Rs. 25,000, and Rs. 20,000 in cash for constructing a retaining wall were contributed by the local people. In appreciation of the work, the district administration contributed funds through the village panchayat under the Self-Sufficiency Scheme to complete the modernisation of the pond. The pond is open to all caste groups including Scheduled Castes. Around 600 families are benefited by this pond. Even in summer the people are able to get water from the pond. But the people are not aware of the need for boiling the water before drinking. Instead, they use a variety of locally available nuts to cleanse the water. Because of the LCO, the land area around the pond and the streams leading to the pond are kept clean. Separate ponds have been reserved in the village for the use of animals and for bathing and washing purposes. The existence of the LCO in the village has contributed to the healthy upkeep of the natural resources with the cooperation of the village panchayat.

PULIKANMAI VILLAGE

Paruthikanmai is a village panchayat in Kalayarkovil Panchayat Union of Sivagangai District. Pulikanmai is a village taken for the study, located in Paruthikanmai village panchayat. The village is located two kms South-West of Kalayarkovil Town. The village is well connected by a road with Kalayarkovil Town and Sivagangai Town.

Ecological Profile

The village has sandy porous soil. The local people call their area *Mankala Nadu*, which in Tamil means sandy soil country. Due to the sandy and porous nature of the soil, its water and moisture retention capacity is very low. Even after heavy rains no water is retained in the land. Because of this, rainfed agriculture is very difficult.[28] The rain in the area is scarce, sporadic and seasonal. The ground water available is also meagre and mostly saline. The tank is the main source of irrigation and there is a tank, namely Pulikanmai. The tank is considered the most valuable resource of the village. Even for drinking water the people depend on the wells in the tank bed and the wells near the tank bunds. For agricultural purposes too, they mainly depend on the tank.

Until the recent past, the people of this village were getting drinking water from the village drinking water ponds. But the practice was discontinued because of growing awareness, education and the availability of potable water from the wells in the tank area.

The Pulikanmai irrigation tank has an irrigated area of 83 acres. The water bed of the tank is 94 acres.[29] The tank has two sluices or water supply regulators through which the tank water is supplied to the fields. The regulator once had wooden shutters and, in the year 1954, the wooden shutters were replaced by steel shutters by the Public Works Department. The first regulator is to supply water to 44 acres and the second regulator is to supply water to 39 acres.[30] The first one is an upper sluice and the second one is a lower sluice. The lower sluice can supply water much more efficiently and for a longer period because of its location at a lower level.

The tank has three wells in the tank bed. Two of them are used for supplementing the tank water in times of scarcity. There are three private wells in the tank irrigated area with limited water source. One well is used by the villagers for drinking water purpose. In addition there is a borewell in the tank bed. It is used by the village panchayat to supply protected drinking water to the village. People prefer to collect water from the open well located in the tank bed because of the sweetness of the water. Out of the two wells in the tank bed used for irrigation one well was dug through the collective efforts of the people some thirty years back to supplement the tank water. The effort of the village was supported by a non-governmental agency. The second well was an outcome of the community well scheme of the government. The second well has been fitted with an electric motor and the water drawn is supplied to the fields. Both the wells are under the control of the LCO. The village has four other small irrigation tanks with an average irrigated area of 15 acres each.[31]

The village has three major ponds and numerous small ponds. Twenty years ago a pond was desilted and protection walls were constructed by the LCO.[32] The idea was to use the pond as a source of drinking water. Now the pond is not used for drinking water, but only for bathing and washing purposes. Two other ponds are used for animals. The tank is used for irrigation for four to five months between September and December. In summer the tank bed is used for grazing. The tank bed and other areas of the village are thickly covered with bushes and trees. The entire tank bed in Pulikanmai is covered by a lush growth of trees. The villagers of Pulikanmai believe that the thick cover of vegetation prevents soil erosion and is useful for free flow of rain water to the tank. They also believe that the thick tree cover induces rain in the area. The tank bunds, the roads and the pathways have trees like neem, udai and banyan. Most of the houses, cattle sheds, wells and ponds are surrounded by a variety of trees. The village has a large number of tamarind trees, mostly in private lands. Most of the houses have at least one tamarind tree. Many houses have two to four tamarind trees. Farmers have planted tamarind trees in their fields too. Tamarind trees are a rich source of income. As a large area is not under cultivation thorny bushes are abundant. A large number of peacocks are spotted in the tank area and in the wastelands around the village.

The supply channels to the tank and other water bodies of the village are cleared and maintained well. There are three main supply channels to the Pulikanmai tank and there are numerous streams for the flow of rain water to the various water bodies in the village.

Socio-Economic Setting

The village has a population of 850 out of whom 158 (18.6 per cent) are SC people.[33] The majority of the people in the village are udayar Christians. The udayars converted to Christianity two hundred years ago. Udayars are mainly a farming community. Even though they are Christians, they keep their caste identity intact. They do not have marriage alliance with other castes. They do not normally mingle freely with the SC people of the village.[34] They have marriage alliance with Hindu udayars. There are 121 Christian udayar families, two maravar families, 32 families of pallars of Scheduled Caste, two families of carpenters, two families of washermen and two families of barbers.[35] Maravars are farmers who once were warriors. The pallars traditionally worked in the fields of others and did not have land. But in Pulikanmai five pallar families have own lands in the tank irrigated area and seven pallar families have land on lease. But most of the pallar community people are landless labourers. In Pulikanmai village economic disparities are not wide. No single individual has more than six acres of land in the tank area.[36]

On investigation it is found that the majority of the families have land in the tank irrigated area.[37] The minimum possession of irrigated land is twenty cents and the maximum is six acres.[38] Most of the families depend on agriculture and only twelve families have people employed outside the village with government and private sector.[39] The area is industrially backward and the village has no economic enterprise other than agriculture. The marginal farming families and the landless in the village work as agricultural labourers. There are 25 families without land.[40] The wages in the agriculture sector for men is Rs. 45 and Rs. 20 for women per day. During harvest time, wages are given in the form of paddy and such wages are relatively high. The labourers form themselves into groups and undertake harvesting and threshing work on contract basis for the farmers. During the harvest season men get around 15 kgs of paddy per day and women get around 10 kgs of paddy. In fifteen to twenty days each family gathers around 300 to 400 kgs of paddy during the harvest season. The service communities also can collect a considerable quantum of paddy for their services provided to the farming community.

The village has a church and a temple. The Scheduled Caste have their own place of worship. There are no separate streets for different communities in this village other than that for the SC families, who live separately in a colony constructed by the government. The village does not have any traditional leaders now. Instead the management of community affairs is looked after by the LCO. The participation of the SC people in the LCO is restricted. There are no caste conflicts in the village. Every year a community feast is arranged near the tank in which the entire village, including the SC people, participate. People have faith that the practice of community feast will ensure proper rains and good harvest to the

COMMUNITY DRINKING WATER POND

PLATE 3.1: A Community Drinking Water Pond maintained by a LCO in Sivagangai District (Susaipattinam Village). The LCO and the village panchayat modernised the pond by their joint efforts. SC people are also using the pond without any restrictions. Two SC girls are seen in the picture. It shows the adaptability of the LCO to the changing social realities.

TREES IN THE COMMON LANDS

PLATE 3.6: Rich growth of trees in the road sides of Pulikanmai.

PLATE 3.7: Growth of trees in the tank bund of Periyakannanur.

village. The SC people also participate without any restriction in this feast.[41]

The activities of political parties are restricted in Pulikanmai village. Party flags, party posters and party meetings are strictly prohibited in the village. Political leaders can visit the village and have informal interaction with the people.[42] The villagers fear that electoral conflicts among various political groups may disturb the unity and stability of the village.

Being a Christian village and due to Christian missionary activities people are educated and well informed. The village has a secondary school, upto the eighth standard. It has a noon meal centre, a library and a ration shop. There are four tractors in the village and many houses have television sets and radios. Like men, the women are also educated. From this small village, five women have been sent to the Vatican as nuns by the efforts of the local church. A young man, with an MBA degree, is working in the Star TV as an executive. The socio-economic background of the village shows that the village has no economic and social conflicts and that the caste system is not oppressive. The villagers are dependent on the irrigation tank for agriculture and employment opportunities. There is perfect communal harmony and there is no caste based exploitation and conflict.

Local Community Organisation

Like many other villages of Kalayarkovil Block in Sivagangai district, Pulikanmai Village has an LCO.[43] In its records, the organisation's name is recorded as Village Common Welfare Association. As per the oral history the organisation has been functionng for decades without any instability. Before 1977, traditional leaders from specific families formed the executive of the village as a hereditary practice. In the year 1977, the traditional leaders decided to introduce a new system of selection of the executive committee for a tenure of one year. The restructured system was introduced in the year 1977. Since 1977 the accounts of the committee have been properly maintained and they were made available for this study.[44]

Kudi System

The basic unit of the organisation is the *kudi* or family. *Kudi*, in the village, means a family which is residing in the village permanently and which is recognised as a member of the village by the village assembly.[45] Two types of membership are available. Families having land are called *vivasaya kudi* (farming family) and families without land are called *podhu kudi* (general family). *Kudi* is defined as a married couple living in the village at least for one year in a joint family or as a nuclear family. Unmarried adults living separately are taken as half *kudi*. Widows with children are considered full *kudi*. The definition of *kudi* is interpreted by the village assembly on requirement.[46] The landowning SC families are also taken into the *kudi* system as faming kudis.[47] However the non-landowning SC families are not entered in the *kudi* system.[48] However, they participate in many other activities of the LCO like any other general kudi member.[49] There is a kudi register in which the membership of the *kudi* is registered.[50]

Normally new kudis are admitted in the month of September. In September the new executive committee takes over the responsibilities from the old one.[51] The *vivasaya kudis* are required to contribute cash, grain and labour for the maintenance of the irrigation tank and for the general village fund. The general *kudis* are required to contribute towards only the general village fund. Most of the *kudis* are farming kudis and there are only five general *kudis* in the village. General *kudis* have all the privileges of all the common facilities and resources except a share in the water in the tank. Farming kudis get a share in the water in the tank and contribute towards its maintenance.

Village Assembly

The village assembly consists of the representatives of the *kudis* in the village, both the general and the farming *kudis*. Meetings are held eight to ten times in a year. In 1996-97, a total of eight meetings were conducted.[52] Attendance of representatives is compulsory and failure without proper reason invites penalty.[53] The meetings are held in an open ground and normally in the evening hours. Notice about the meeting is given at least two days in advance. The executive committee members decide the date and the time of the meeting and the general agenda. The President of the executive committee presides over the meetings. Normally women do not participate in the meeting. But, on requirement, women can present their views, demands and requests in the general assembly. Participation by the SC people is very limited. The landowning SC families participate in the meetings on matters related to tank water management. If landless SC families want to speak in the village assembly, they have to get permission from the President. They have to pay Rs. 2 to the common fund for presenting their case before the assembly, because they do not ordinarily contribute to the common fund.[54] The village assembly has the following functions:[55]

1. Admitting members as *kudis* into the organisation.
2. Selection of executive committee.
3. Fixing contributions from the members.
4. Framing the cropping calender.
5. Fixing dates for kudimaramathu, raising nursery, opening and closing of sluices, and, temple festivals.
6. Auctioning fisheries and grazing rights.
7. Appointment of common irrigators, watch and ward staff and fixing their salaries.
8. Control over village common fund.
9. Sanctioning expenditure from common fund.
10. Welfare and development activities of the village.
11. General control over common property resources.

Decisions are taken long discussions and by consensus in the general assembly. There is no practice of taking decisions by voting. Normally the village elders guide discussions and negotiate among conflicting interests to bring about compromise.

Executive Committee

The village assembly selects a five-members executive committee for one year's tenure.[56] The committee members are changed by the village assembly in the month of September. Normally there is no contest for executive committee membership and selection is based on consensus. Before 1977 the traditional leaders formed the executive body on a permanent basis. In 1977 the system of selection of executive committee members by the village assembly for a period of one year on rotation among all the members was introduced. From among the five members, the President and the Secretary are selected by the village assembly. A joint bank account is opened in the name of three senior members. The accounts are maintained by the Secretary. The major activities of the executive committee are:[57]

1. Convening village assembly meetings.
2. Implementing the decisions taken by the village assembly.
3. Exercising control over the staff of the LCO.
4. Operating the village common fund.
5. Maintaining the accounts of the assembly.
6. Collecting contributions from the members.
7. Attending to emergency functions.
8. Receiving representations from the villagers.
9. Looking after the general welfare of the village.
10. Representing the village to the government and other agencies.

The President of the present committee is a retired teacher and a progressive farmer. He has a tractor and a number of cattle. He owns four acres of wet land in the tank irrigated area. One of his daughters is a nun serving in Vatican City.[58] He is considered honest and sincere in activities related to the village. The executive committee is authorised to keep Rs. 500 as cash on hand from the village common fund and spend upto Rs. 200 without sanction from the village assembly.[59] The executive members regularly interact among themselves and with the people of the village. Problems are quickly discussed and solutions are arrived at. Special meetings of the village assembly are arranged in emergencies by the executive committee.

Participation Facilitated by the LCO

(a) Participation in Kudimaramathu

As in many other villages in Sivagangai and Ramnad districts, the people in Pulikanmai village regularly undertake kudimaramathu. *Vivasaya kudis* in the village take the responsibility of doing kudimaramathu. Kudimaramathu in the village has the following functions:[60]

1. Clearance of supply channels
2. Desilting the sluice areas
3. Clearance of field channels.

Before the onset of the monsoon, a special meeting to discuss kudimaramathu work is conducted. The meeting decides the date and the time of the work.

Normally the clearing of the supply channels is done in the month of August. For the annual clearance work every *kudi* has to contribute labour. Every *vivasaya kudi* has to send one person with required implements like spade, basket, pan and crowbar for the work. Both men and women are accepted. In case a *kudi* is not in a position to send a person it can send a labourer as an alternative. On the same day the silt around the sluices of the supply channels are removed and it is ensured that the sluice is in good condition. In one single day the clearance work is done.Clearance of the field channels is also done on a fixed day before the opening of the sluices.

(b) Participation in Emergency Repair of Tank

During the rainy season and floods, the entire Pulikanmai village carefully watches the flood situation. The common irrigators, farmers and executive committee members take great care to prevent breaches. In case of overflow of water, specific methods are vailable as precautionary measures. In the year 1995, there was a breach in the tank.[61] All the families were asked to come to work with empty jute bags. Each family was required to bring at least two such jute bags. Around two hundred men, women and children were engaged to repair the breach in the tank. Around three hundred jute bags filled with sand were used in the operation. Within four hours the entire operation was over. The cost of the operation could be around ten thousand rupees.[62] It is impossible for any state agency or panchayat to meet such an emergency situation mustering people's participation.

(c) Participation in Distribution of Water

Water is a scarce commodity in Pulikanmai village. The water in the tank has to be economically used and coordination among the users is required to save water. In case there is no control over the use of water, chances for crop failure are high. In view of this the farmers of Pulikanmai have a practice of taking collective decisions regarding water in their village assembly.[63] The village assembly decides the date for opening the sluices. It appoints two common irrigators. Appointment of common irrigators helps the people to overcome difficulties in water distribution to the fields. The two irrigators can take care of the irrigation to all the fields served by the tank. Individual farmers are relieved of their responsibility of irrigating their farms. As the common irrigators are experienced people, they can use the water more efficiently and economically than other individuals.

Conflicts over use of water, particularly in times of water scarcity, are also reduced by the presence of the common irrigators. Common irrigators are well aware of the rules, regulations and customs relating to the distribution of water. As the common irrigators have to collect their wages from the farmers, they ensure proper water distribution. The performance of the common irrigators is also monitored by the farmers and deficiencies, if any, are reported promptly to the executive committee.

(d) Participation in Scarcity Management

Water scarcity is a frequent problem in Pulikanmai. Water scarcity may result in damage to the standing crops. To manage water scarcity, the people of Pulikanmai have developed from experience a method of management.[64] Food security and equity are the two basic principles governing the strategy for managing water scarcity. Water is considered a common property of the village and every *kudi* is assured minimum water supply to ensure minimum harvest. To manage acute water scarcity, special village assembly meetings are held. Depending on the availability of water, the area to be cultivated is determined. If the tank is filled only to half its capacity, normally the assembly allows the farmers to cultivate only 50 per cent of the landholding of the *kudis*. *Kudis* having less than 50 cents are permitted to irrigate their entire land area. If the water scarcity is acute, another system *viz*., *Kudi Eevu* or share of the *kudi* is followed. In this system the concept of equity in water use is followed. Each *kudi* is permitted to irrigate only a small piece of land (about 50 cents) to ensure fulfilment of minimum food requirement for the year. The size of the landholding of the individual is not taken into consideration. In this system small and marginal farmers are benefited. But indirectly, the large farmers are also benefited, because unregulated use of water without any planning at a time of water scarcity may result in crop failure and economic loss. The theoretical problem of Hardin's tragedy of commons is skilfully avoided by the participatory approach of the *kudi* system of Pulikanmai.

(e) Participation in Community Fishing

As per the rules the right to harvest fish in the panchayat irrigation works must be given on lease to generate income for the panchayat. In Pulikanmai village, the LCO has taken the responsibility of using the irrigation tank in the village to regulate fishing in the tank for the benfit of the entire community.[65] Individual fishing or unauthorised fishing in the tank is strictly prohibited.

The executive committee members negotiate with the panchayat and, as per the government rule, they pay the minimum fee prescribed and avoid public auction. On a date fixed by the village assembly, the tank is opened for community fishing. A member from each *kudi* is permitted to enter the tank for fish harvesting. Within three hours the harvest can be completed. The next day onwards people are allowed to fish in the tank without any restriction. For nearly a week people can get fish for personal use. The system regulates the behaviour of the community for the entire year and permits them to harvest the benefit collectively by the year end. Every family in the village gets fish for nearly a week in a year.

(f) Participation in Conservation of Trees

The people of Pulikanmai are aware of the importance of conservation of the watershed for the health of the irrigation tanks and the ecology of the village. Conservation of trees and the regulation of grazing are the twin policies followed by the LCO. The trees in the tank and in the *poramboke* lands are under the control of various government departments, the panchayat and the panchayat union. But, in Pulikanmai, regulations have been imposed by the LCO to conserve the trees in the village. Two guards have been appointed in the village to prevent any unauthorised cutting of trees. The entire village has taken the responsibility of protecting the trees. Any unauthorised cutting attracts penalty by the village assembly.[66] Abundant thorny bushes are available in the *poramboke* lands of the village for fuel for the people of the village.

(g) Participation in Regulation of Grazing

The LCO has imposed restrictions on grazing[67] to conserve the top soil, to avoid silting of the tank and for the conservation of plants. Such restrictions are discussed in the village assembly and decisions are taken. At present, the following two types of restrictions are imposed on grazing:

1. Rearing or grazing of goat is strictly prohibited within the village land area.
2. Grazing permits are issued by the LCO for cattle other than goats.

Goat rearing is a profitable income generating activity in rural areas. Pulikanmai village has abundant vegetation which is favourable for goat rearing. But the villagers have collectively imposed a ban on goat rearing, as goat rearing is considered a great threat to top soil, vegetation and conservation of trees.

Grazing by other animals is also restricted and stall feeding is practised in the village. During summer, when getting fodder is difficult grazing permits are issued to cattle other than goats. From this practice the village generates resource for the local community fund. In the year 1996-97, the village could collect around Rs. 5,000 from issuing permits for grazing.[68] By issuing permits, the community organisation can restrict the number of animals, types of animals and duration of grazing in a year. People strictly follow the rules relating goats. If a goat is purchased for the purpose of meat, it cannot be kept by a household for more than a week. Violation of this rule will attract penalty.

(h) Participation in Collective Good

Wade argues, "In the South Indian context at least, villagers are likely to follow joint rules and arrangements only to achieve intensely felt needs that could not be met by individual response. These are likely to be concerned primarily with the defense of production (avoidance of crop or animal loss) secondarily with the enhancement of income, and finally (and a long stretch from the first two) with education, nutrition, health and civic consciousness."[69]

The LCO, which is primarily concerned with the management of natural resources is also able to generate participation in the form of labour contribution, monetary contribution and adherence to prescribed rules for the development of the village in the following areas.

The villagers of Pulikanmai have decided to ban liquor (sale or use) within the boundaries of the village. The mismanagement of the Government run noon meal centre was collectively challenged by the people. The LCO tried to correct the corrupt organiser of the noon meal centre by persuasion. The food materials and eggs of the centre were not properly distributed to local children by the corrupt noon meal organiser who had political patronage. The LCO repeatedly made several representations to the higher officials and finally got the noon meal organiser transferred from the village. Around Rs. 700 was spent from the village common fund for getting this transfer.[70] The village did not have a ration shop. The villagers had to walk two kilometres to collect their ration goods from a nearby village. The village assembly decided to take efforts to bring a ration shop to the village and authorised the executive committee to take necessary steps and to spend money for the purpose from the village common fund. The executive committee worked hard for nearly two years to get sanction for the ration shop. A sum of Rs. 1,600 was spent from the village common fund for this common purpose.[71]

A local library and reading room was a felt need in the village. In a meeting of the village assembly it was decided to get a government sponsored local library in the village. For starting a local library, as per government rule, a minimum number of people have to take membership by paying the prescribed fee and the local community has to contribute a share of the expenditure on establishing a library.

The village assembly spend Rs. 22,000 on the supply of chairs, tables, books and payment of membership fee.[72] Within fifteen days all the requirements for starting a rural library were fulfilled by the LCO.

In the same way, the village has constructed a building in the local secondary school by its efforts. The *kudis* were asked to provide a person each to work in the construction project. The expenses on materials for the construction were met from the village common fund. Around Rs. 15,000 worth of materials and Rs. 10,000 worth of a labour were contributed towards the construction of the school building.[73]

The village has the practice of collectively contributing for the funeral ceremony of anyone dying in the village. In case of a death, every *kudi* has to pay Rs. 10 each and around Rs. 1,200 is immediately mobilised. The collection is given to the bereaved family. At least one member from each *kudi* has to attend the funeral ceremony. It is an arrangement of social security and displays communal solidarity. Such social action brings people together and personal conflicts and differences of opinion among families are reduced by such repeated processes of community action. It builds a base for harmony and cooperation among families for development work.

The LCO of Pulikanmai also operates a micro credit system. The major portion of the community fund is offered for credit to its members. In the year 1996-97, Rs. 25,000 was distributed from the community fund among 50 *kudis* at an interest rate of 36 per cent.[74] As the interest rate was high, only people with real need took the loan and repayment was very prompt. The income generated from the credit system was recycled again and again into the credit system. Normally the commercial money lender charged not less than 60 per cent. The common fund in the village now gives a helping hand to the families in the village during emergencies and saves them from the clutches of money lenders.

Assurance Provided by the LCO

As discussed earlier, 'assurance' is the key factor in facilitating collective action for the management of natural resources. Institutions are required to coordinate and predict the behaviour of individuals in the context of collective action.

If an institution can give sufficient assurance and if the participants are profited by their contribution, the scope for participation is high. In Pulikanmai village the farmers want to avoid crop failure due to water scarcity. Use of water without any restriction or coordination may result in crop loss. Such crop loss will ruin their economy. This is a key factor which influences the people of Pulikanmai to enter into an institutional framework. As per the law, the tank has to be managed and water has to be distributed by the panchayats. But, in practice, not only in Pulikanmai, but also all over Tamil Nadu, the panchayats do not undertake any such work.

In Pulikanmai, under threat of economic loss, people have developed a regulation of behaviour and an institutional arrangement to coordinate behaviour. Their organisation gives them assurance on efficient management of water. For managing scarcity of water and avoiding risk of crop failure, they depend on their organisation. The organisation, its rules and its conventions, are developed locally by the beneficiaries or stake holders over a period of time. The organisation is fully autonomous. People are sure that their organisation is not controlled by any other outside agency. The organisation ensures that none-contributors are not permitted to enjoy common benefits created out of the contribution of the rule abiding participants and no one can enjoy a free ride. The organisation is controlled by the stake holders and all major decisions are taken by them. The primary concern is the protection of the interests of the stake holders. The supply of water as per the rules to the fields of the participants is ensured by the organisation. Appointment of common irrigators reduces the expenses of the individual farmers. It also prevents conflicts among farmers in water sharing. The *kudi* system links contribution to resource sharing. Without contributing to the maintenance of the irrigation tank, one cannot get water from the tank. This assurance by the institution ensures a positive behaviour among the participants conducive to cooperation for collective good.

Another important assurance given by the institution is that of equal distribution of water among all *kudis* in case of scarcity. The interest of marginal farmers is also protected by this scheme. Every *kudi* is assured of minimum harvest of paddy even in a year of water scarcity. In the absence of such regulation, the entire crop in the tank area may fail in years of water scarcity.

The processes of decision-making and implementation are very simple, transparent and quick enough to meet the requirements of the people. As there is no separate official machinery for this work, the cost of transactions is minimum and the scope for corruption is limited. As sanction for expenditure is given by the village assembly and the accounts of the organisation are discussed in the village assembly the scope for any misappropriation of funds is also nearly eliminated. The account books are well maintained. As the executive committee has only one year's tenure and membership is rotated, there is no scope for dominance by any individual in organisational matters.

The system has been operating efficiently for several decades. The present structure of the organisation is a modernised form of the older organisation. In the new structure, traditional leaders have been replaced by an executive committee selected for one year. There is no electoral politics in the organisation and there is no intervention by any government authority. Because of these reasons the organisation is stable. This stability gives assurance to the individuals on the predictable behaviour of the organisation.

The most important strength of the local organisation is the capacity to conserve and sustain natural resources for several generations. Because of the proper maintenance of the irrigation tank and other water bodies the people of the village are assured of getting the minimum harvest.

The assurance given by LCO facilitates and sustains the participation of the people of Pulikanmai in the management of natural resources.

Samples from the Records of Income and Expenditure of Pulikanmai for the Year 1988-89[75]
(Illustrative Examples)

Income		*Amount (in Rs.)*
1.	Fine for an individual who did not attend the village assembly meeting	1.00
2.	Fine for not providing labour in the school construction activity	10.00
3.	Fine for unauthorised use of tank water and wasting of water	10.00
4.	Fine for stealing a hen—Rs. 75. (Out of this Rs. 25 was paid to the owner of the hen)	50.00
5.	Fine for grazing goat in the tank bed Rs. 50. (Out of this Rs. 25 was paid to the informer)	25.00
6.	Fine for unauthorised use of tank water on 13 persons (@ Rs. 30 each)	390.00
7.	Income from sale of two towels remaining	

	after a function organised for opening of the new school building	15.00
8.	Income for issuing four permits for grazing (@ Rs. 300 each)	1200.00
9.	Income from renting out the vessels of the community organisation for a marriage	570.00
10.	Balance amount from the community feeding programme for rain.	242.00

	Expenditure	*Amount (in Rs.)*
1.	Expenditure on the representatives' visit to the District Collector Office to correct a mistake in the land re-survey conducted in the village by the Land Revenue Department (for four persons)	23.10
2.	Expenditure on a trip to the District Collector's Office for getting saction for a ration shop in the village (for four persons)	50.00
3.	Expenditure on repair of electric motor in the community well in the tank	200.00
4.	Labour charges for clearing a supply channel	48.00
5.	Expenditure on purchase of pumping and electrical goods for the community well in the tank	1500.00
6.	Expenditure on the purchase of match boxes	1.50

Samples from Records of Income and Expenditure for the Year 1996-97[76]

(Illustrative Examples)

	Income	*Amount (in Rs.)*
1.	Income from repayment of credit and interest from 47 *kudis*	29,240.00
2.	Income from issue of grazing permits	2,500.00
3.	Income from permitting construction of a memorial in the graveyard	500.00

4.	Fine for damaging the kalingu (a tank structure) on two individuals from a nearby village	500.00
5.	Issue of grazing permit	100.00
6.	Issue of grazing permit	2,000.00
7.	Income from sale of thorny bushes in the tank area.	7,500.00

	Expenditure	*Amount (in Rs.)*
1.	Expenditure on building, chairs and books for the local library	20,000.00
2.	Expenditure on trip to the District Collector's Office for transferring a corrupt organiser of Noon Meal Centre of the village	24.00
3.	Engaging labour for clearnace of supply channels of the tank	500.00
4.	Expenditure on opening ceremony of the new ration shop	530.00
5.	Expenditure on payment towards membership fee in the local library for 100 persons (Rs. 20 per head).	2,000.00

Details of Income and Expenditure of the Local Community Organisation of Pulikanmai Village[77]

The income and expenditure for the year 1996-97

Income	Rs. 53,716.00
Expenditure	Rs. 26,133.00
Balance	Rs. 27,583.00

The income and expenditure for the year 1997-98

Balance from the previous year	Rs. 27,583.00
Income	Rs. 58,241.00
Total	Rs. 85,824.00
Expenditure	Rs. 6,723.00
Balance	Rs. 79,161.00

Participation and Panchayat

Paruthikanmai village panchayat has one main village namely Pulikanmai and three other hamlets. The village panchayat has six members. Out of the six member seats, two are reserved for women and one is reserved for the Scheduled Caste. But the actual position is that there are three women members and two SC members (one SC male and one SC female). Out of the six, four belong to the backward class (BC). The panchayat union ward council member from the area is a BC male.

Position of Village Panchayat Members[78]

As per Rule			*Actual Position*		
General	—	3	General Male	—	2
Female	—	2	Female	—	3 (1 SC)
SC General	—	1	SC Male	—	1

(One SC female is elected from the general ward of Pulikanmai village because of the initiative of the LCO).

The panchayat union and village panchayat, as per the information available from the records, have not undertaken any effort to mobilise people's participation in the management of the irrigation tank. Kudimaramathu, compulsory labour contribution for emergency repair of tank structure, distribution of water, scarcity management of water, development of trees in the tank area, protection of trees in the *poramboke* lands and regulation of grazing are some of the functions the panchayat union and the village panchayat can undertake. A careful study of the records reveal the fact that, in the last two and half years, the panchayats have not mobilised people's participation for the above mentioned purposes in Pulikanmai village.[79]

According to the President of the village panchayat, the village panchayat mainly concentrates on providing the obligatory services like providing drinking water and maintenance of street lights.[80]

People expect only such things from the village panchayat. Another important service provided by the village panchayat is operation of the television sets in the villages. The village panchayat has two overhead tanks and 19 hand pumps for supply of drinking water. It maintains 69 street lights. The panchayat maintains 4 km of local road. There is a public telephone provided by the Telecommunication Department in a common place.

The village panchayat has to spend a major portion of its revenue on maintaining the above mentioned facilities.[81] In the year 1997-98, out of the total revenue of Rs. 96,574 the village panchayat spent Rs. 60,095 on street lights and water supply. In the year 1996-97 and 1997-98, the panchayat has not undertaken any work related to the development of water bodies or any natural resources.[82] Government grant is the only major income for the panchayat. In the year 1997-98, out of the total income of Rs. 96,574. Rs. 51,894 came from the government as grant on the recommendation of the State Finance Commission and Rs. 23,119 came from the transactions of land registration. So, around 80 per cent of the income of the village panchayat comes from outside agencies.[83]

The panchayat has not mobilised any resource locally from the Local Common Property Resources in the last three years. Even the money received under the Jawahar Rozgar Yojana was used for construction of a television room, a bus stop and on improvement of local roads. Only Rs. 13,900 was spent on the construction of the retention wall of a village pond in a hamlet. The village panchayat did not make any attempt to mobilise people's participation in the above programmes.[84]

The Gram Sabha of the panchayat was also not able to generate any enthusiasm among the people. The meetings did not discuss any matter related to the management of natural resources.[85]

In the meetings of the village panchayat too, no serious matters relating to natural resource management with people's participation were taken up for discussion. Most of the resolutions were related to spending of the panchayat money for providing facilities to the local people.[86] Not only in the village panchayat but also in the panchayat union council, matters relating to involvement of local people in the management of natural resources with reference to irrigation tanks were not discussed. In Pulikanmai village, the panchayat union did not spend any money on development of the irrigation tank. It also did not generate any income from the panchayat union tank in the last three years.[87] The panchayat union council member from the area also did not take any initiative to involve the local people in the development of the irrigation tank and other resources related to it in Pulikanmai village.

The village panchayat President expressed his view that panchayati raj institutions were not practically empowered to take the required steps to involve the local people in the management of natural resources. Even if the people are ready to cooperate, the procedures and rules of the Government are not conducive to effective participation.

The panchayat President himself is not clear about the rules and regulations relating to the management of natural resources in the village. According to him, involvement of too many departments in the process has made the task very complex and very difficult.

Process of Accommodating the LCO

The LCO of Pulikanmai village is working effectively in the village for several decades and it is not possible for the village panchayat to ignore it. In fact, at the time of the panchayat elections, the village assembly evolved a consensus candidate for the post of President. Out of the two seats reserved for women among the Pulikanmai general wards, one was given to the SC people of the village as a token of goodwill. As a result, even though only one seat was reserved for the Scheduled Caste, additionally one SC female was elected from a general ward of Pulikanmai village. The panchayat President and the other members from Pulikanmai are very positive towards the LCO. The President of the village panchayat concentrates mostly on activities relating to municipal services, programmes for people below poverty line and self-employment schemes. The LCO came forward to deepen and repair a drinking water well in the tank bed. The LCO was ready to spend Rs. 10,000 and mobilised labour for the task. The village panchayat could sanction Rs. 12,000 for this work.[88] By collective action around Rs. 22,000 was spent. It is an example of joint management by community based organisation and panchayati raj institution.

Pulikanmai has a rich growth of useful trees like neem in public lands. The village *poramboke* land is fully covered with wild growth of trees, bushes and vegetation. The village panchayat has the responsibility to protect all these. But it has no manpower to do so. The LCO has appointed two guards to protect the trees in the village. The LCO has also taken the responsibility of strictly regulating grazing in the village common land. The LCO has banned grazing by goats and issues permits to other cattle owners to taken them for grazing in the common land. These regulations save plants not only in public lands but also in private lands. Such regulations cannot be imposed by the panchayats. But the LCO has been able to do so with great success.

Regular kudimaramathu work is being organised by the LCO in the panchayat union irrigation tank. During floods and emergencies, only the LCO protects the tank structures. Some of the activities mentioned in the 73rd Constitutional Amendment Act (243G) are undertaken by the LCO in Pulikanmai village. As discussed earlier, the LCO contributed to the improvement of the village school and noon meal centre. Even though the village panchayat and the panchayat union can legally involve themselves in such activities, practically they are not doing so. The establishment of a local library was the most important contribution of the LCO in the year 1997-98. There was frequent voltage drop in the electricity supply to the village. The LCO paid money to the Electricity Board to meet additional expenditure for improving the power supply to the village. Such activities cannot be undertaken by the village panchayats, even though the street lights maintained by the village panchayats are affected by the voltage drop.

The President of the village panchayat considers the LCO a source of strength for the panchayat. The panchayat President is consulted by the LCO in all matters relating to community welfare. The panchayat and LCO are able to collectively solve many problems of the people of the village of Pulikanmai.

PERIYAKANNANUR

Socio-Economic Setting

Periyakannanur village is located in the Kalayarkovil panchayat union of Sivagangai district in Tamil Nadu State. The village is located 14 km south of Sivagangai Town. The village is well connected with the district headquarters by road. Periyakannanur Village Panchayat has a population of 1812, of which 307 belong to the Scheduled Caste.[89] The village panchayat has 11 hamlets and Periyakannanur is the main village with a population of 1082. Out of them 284 belong to the Scheduled Caste.[90] The village has 242 families, out of which 81 belong to the maravar community, who are traditionally farmers. There are 56 yadava families, who are traditionally herdsmen and have now become farmers. There are fifteen Muslim, five barber, four washermen, three vellalar, two carpenter and four priest families.[91] Out of the 242 families, 70 belong to the Scheduled Caste, and 172 belong to the backward class. Nearly one-third of the families belong to the Scheduled Caste, who have their own colony near the village. The village is socially heterogeneous without any domination by any single caste. The fifteen Muslim families in the village speak Tamil and maintain full identity with the other groups in the village.

Most of the families are small and marginal farmers and they own land ranging from 30 cents to 5 acres.[92] Only twenty families have more than 5 acres.[93] All the families are primarily farmers. There are five families engaged in small business like petty shop, grocery shop and tea shop.

The lands in the village were once owned by twelve brahmin and mudhaliyar families. The BC and the SC families were working on their lands as tenants. In the year 1952, the Tamil Nadu Peasant Association, a wing of the Communist Party of India, started a branch in the village to protect the interests of the peasants. After prolonged struggle for a decade, the land owners decided to sell their lands to the peasants against nominal payment. The Peasant Association in the village ensured the transfer of the land to the peasants in an equitable manner to benefit every section of the community including the SC families. In this struggle hundreds of families had to suffer and many of the villagers went to prison. Land transfer was achieved in the village by legal battle, social pressure, political struggle and prolonged negotiation.[94]

Because of the historical background of the village, leftist political influence is still prevalent in the village. It has brought about significant change in the social relationship between different caste groups. All SC families have land for cultivation.[95] Like all others the SC families participate in the affairs of the village and there are no incidents of atrocity against them. The Muslims of the village also have land and freely mingle with the other caste groups. They participate even in the Hindu religious festivals of the village.

Ecological Profile of the Village

Periyakannanur village has sandy light soil without moisture and water retention capacity. The rains are seasonal, scarce and sporadic. The ground water is saline. The saline ground water is not suitable for irrigation. There are no wells used for agriculture. The village has a panchayat union tank, and a PWD tank. In addition, the village has a large number of streams and ponds in the watershed area. The village has four major ponds. Two of them are used for bathing and cleaning purposes. The other two are used for animals. The village does not have any land under rainfed farming. Except the tank irrigated area other land areas are left fallow. These land areas are covered densely with bushes, trees and thorny plants.

The PWD tank has 452 acres of irrigation area. It has four sluices.[96] The panchayat union tank has 96 acres of irrigated area and has two sluices.[97] The panchayat union tank and the PWD tank belong to the same watershed. They have the same water supply source. Only after the PWD tank is filled, water flows to the panchayat union tank. This makes for possible confusion. In a natural watershed, there is need for an integral approach to water harvesting, soil conservation, conservation of vegetation and use of water.

Normally the tanks are filled in the month of September or October by the rains of the North-East monsoon. The water is stored for nearly four months for irrigation and used economically.

In Periyakannanur village, the supply channel and field channels are kept clean to facilitate better harvesting of the available scarce rain water. The watershed area of the tank is densely covered by vegetation. It helps to conserve the top soil and to reduce soil erosion. The control of soil erosion reduces the siltation of the tank bed. Siltation of the tank bed is a threat because it will reduce the water storing capacity of the tank and free flow of the water through the sluices. Restrictions on grazing and banning of goat rearing in the village has had an impact on the tank watershed area. The restrictions have helped the individuals to grow trees in their private land. A variety of useful trees like neem, tamarind, pungam and others are grown around the houses. Almost all the houses have a few trees. Villagers get fuel, fodder and timber from the trees. The trees in the common lands generate income for the village common fund. The water bodies are rich sources of fishing. The community gets fish from the water bodies free of cost for several days in a year.

Local Community Organisation

Like many villages of Sivagangai district, Periyakannanur village has an LCO. The LCO has the following three important structures :

1. *Kudi* System
2. Village Assembly
3. Executive Committee.

The Kudi System

In Periyakannanur village, *kudi* means the families permanently residing in the village and having land in the tank irrigated area. All they families from all caste groups have land in the tank irrigated area and have membership in the *kudi* system. *Kudi* is defined by the village assembly in case of any confusion.

The *kudi* register is opened in the month of December for new registrations. In the year 1998, there were 242 *kudis* in the village. The *kudis* have certain responsibilities and certain rights in the village.[98] The responsibilities of *kudis* include contribution of labour to the annual kudimaramathu, emergency work in the tank, payment for village festivals and adherence to the rules prescribed. In return, they can enjoy certain rights like use of tank water, participation in the village assembly, share in all common resources and participation in village festivals. Membership, duties and rights are interwoven in the *kudi* system. *Kudi* membership gives identity with the village community and it is a form of social security.

The Village Assembly

The village assembly consists of the representatives of the *kudis*.[99] Normally the oldest male of a *kudi* is expected to represent the *kudi* in the village assembly. It is an obligatory duty of the *kudi* to send a representative. But, in practice, more than one member from the *kudi* participates in the meetings. Women also observe the proceedings of the meetings. There is no caste based discrimination in the village assembly and SC members participate like any other members.

The village assembly meetings are held normally at night and in the common ground near the entrance to the village. The date, the time and the venue of the meetings are decided by the President of the LCO in consultation with the elders of the village. The meeting is announced to the public by a drum beater at least one day in advance. The President of the LCO conducts the meeting and there is no special seating arrangement. The President and the elders of the village ensure that the meetings are conducted in an orderly manner. In case of any strong difference of opinion, the elders try to bring the conflicting parties to an understanding. There is no practice of taking decisions by voting. All the decisions are taken only by consensus. The meetings are conducted openly and anyone is free to observe them. Some of the issues normally discussed in the village assembly are given below:[100]

1. Admitting new *kudi* members.

2. Fixing of cropping calender.
3. Opening of sluice of the tank for irrigation.
4. Appointment of common irrigators.
5. Fixing of date for kudimaramathu.
6. Appointing village guard.
7. Framing rules related to distribution of tank water.
8. Management of tank water during scarcity.
9. Verifying the accounts of village common fund.
10. Enquiries related to violation of prescribed rules.
11. Matters related to village festivals.
12. Regulation of grazing in the common area.
13. Regulation of goat rearing.
14. Fixing various types of contributions to be made by the members.
15. Fixing date for community fishing in the tank and other water bodies.
16. Sale or lease of certain common resources for generating revenue for the village common fund.
17. Matters related to development of the village school.
18. Disputes between individuals.

The village assembly takes decisions on issues after thorough discussion. The decisions are taken and announced in the meeting itself. Once the decision in taken, all the members of the assembly are expected to abide by the decision. The executive committee members of the LCO have the responsibility to implement the decisions. Mutual social pressure by the members ensures proper implementation of the decisions without much need for monitoring.

Executive Committee

The village assembly of Periyakannanur takes decisions on the matters listed earlier.[101] Proper execution of the decision requires an executive committee. The village assembly does not periodically elect the members of the executive committee for a fixed tenure. Instead the village assembly has authorised a group of three elders to function as the executive committee. The President of the committee is a seventy-five year old man and has rich experience of public service. He was a key person in the struggle of the peasants for land distribution. Because of his contribution to the struggle, outside contacts, leadership qualities and interest in public welfare, he is selected as the leader of the LCO. The two other members are also selected on the basis of their leadership qualities. The members can be changed by the village assembly based on requirements. But the President has been occupying the office for nearly thirty years.

The executive committee is authorised to operate the community fund. The bank account of the LCO is jointly operated by the members of the executive committee.[102]

The major functions of the executive committee are :

1. Convening the village assembly meeting.
2. Implementing the decisions of the village assembly.
3. Ensuring the conduct of kudimaramathu work.
4. Ensuring contributions from the *kudis*.
5. Supervising of the work of common irrigators and village guards.
6. Organising village festivals.
7. Taking operational decisions related to irrigation tanks.
8. Attending to complaints from the *kudi* members.
9. Operating the common fund.
10. Maintaining the accounts.
11. Maintaining the *kudi* register.
12. Maintaining liaison with government agencies in the common interest.

Participation Facilitated by the LCO

(a) Participation in Maintenance of Tanks

The village assembly decides the date, the time and the duties related to kudimaramathu. Public announcement of kudimaramathu is made well in advance.[103] As the decision makers themselves have to implement the decision, there is no need for coercion. All the *kudis* must send a representative to the kudimaramathu work with the agricultural implements needed for the work. In case any family is not in a position to send a person because of genuine reasons, it must inform the President in advance and must pay labour charges for a substitute. Both males and females are admitted to the work. In practice, apart from the regular participants from the *kudis*, a number of youths and children also take part in the work voluntarily. The channel clearance of the two tanks is undertaken on two different days by the *kudis* having land in the respective tanks. Normally the work starts around 7.30 a.m. in the morning and goes on upto 4.30 p.m.

(b) Participation in Emergency Repairs in Tanks

The Madras Compulsory Labour Act 1858, which is still operational and has been included in the Panchayat Act of 1994, makes it compulsory for the community to repair the tank breaches during floods and in emergencies. The Act of 1994 expects the village panchayat also to attend to the work. But, in practice, neither the village panchayat nor the Revenue Department could engage promptly in such emergency operations. In Periyakannanur village the village assembly has taken the responsibility to monitor the physical structures of the irrigation tanks during floods.[104] The executive committee members, elders, youths, common irrigators and village guards constantly keep on eye on the flood situation. There is an understanding in the community that everyone in the village must report for repair work during breaches and work together to repair the tank structure. In the year 1998, there was a major breach in the PWD tank. The entire village came forward to save the tank bund. Around four hundred people worked together for nearly four hours and repaired the breach.

(c) Participation in Distribution of Water

Distribution of water is very important in Periyakannanur village because water is a scarce resource and it must be used economically without any wastage.[105] The village assembly appoints common irrigators to distribute water to the fields. In Periyakannanur village six common irrigators have been appointed. The appointment is done by the village assembly. The rules of water distribution are evolved mostly from experience. They are time tested and the rules are known to everyone. The members of the *kudi* system are free to watch the performance of the common irrigators and they may bring any deficiency to the notice of the village assembly or the executive committee. The cost of having common irrigators is much less than having separate irrigators for each and every farmer. By virtue of their experience, the common irrigators know how to use the water effectively and economically.

The common irrigators are paid about 15 kg. of paddy per acre of irrigated land. This depends on the yield from the crop. In case of crop failure, the common irrigators are paid very little in the form of cash. So the common irrigators are very much concerned about good harvest and work very hard and sincerely to ensure proper irrigation. In a year of good harvest, a common irrigator may get around 750 kg. of paddy.

(d) Participation in the Management of Water Scarcity

Risk and scarcity, according to Wade, are the key determinants of cooperation among peasants for achieving common good. Because of ecological factors the farmers of Periyakannanur village are always facing water scarcity and risk of crop failure. The people have developed a participatory strategy to solve this problem.[106] The people collectively determine the cropping calendar. In years of very good monsoon no restriction is imposed. In case of water scarcity, the area to be planted is carefully determined collectively in the village assembly to avoid crop failure.

In years of acute scarcity of water, a system called 'sharing of water' is introduced by the village assembly. The village assembly, after carefully studying the availability of water, decides how much area each *kudi* can irrigate. By this process the total area to be irrigated can be restricted according to the availability of water. The guiding principles are :

1. Crop failure must be avoided by saving atleast a portion of the standing crop.
2. Every family in the village must be helped to get at least the minimum food requirement for the family.

For several decades the people of Periyakannanur village have been able to cooperate among themselves to solve water scarcity, which is a common problem. The system is in favour of small and marginal farmers. But it also helps the entire farming community irrespective of the size of their landholding by avoiding total failure of crop and monetary loss. Non-cooperative, individualistic and competitive use of water would bring disaster to the entire farming community in the village. By repeated experiments, the people of Periyakannanur have been able to achieve collective rationality.

(e) Participation in the Community Fish Harvesting

As per the Panchayat Act, fishery is a source of revenue generation for panchayats. The panchayats can generate money by publicly auctioning the fishing rights. But the LCO of Periyakannanur normally makes the minimum payment to the panchayat and organises community fishing.[107] Individual fishing is not allowed and the people, the common irrigators and the village guards check any attempt at fishing by individuals in the water bodies of the village. The village assembly, after the harvest of crops is over, decides the date and the time for community fishing in the tanks. In Periyakannanur the entire fish is harvested collectively on a fixed day and the harvested fish is equally divided among all the *kudis*. After the community harvest, individuals are free to collect fish by individual effort. As the village has two big tanks and numerous ponds, the villagers can get fish for nearly a month after the harvest season without paying anything for it. The poor families of the village are also able to consume fish for nearly a month, which would otherwise be impossible. The community fishing is a symbol of community authority over the fishing rights in the village. The process of marketisation is eliminated and the benefit is shared by all the families.

(f) Participation in the Conservation of Trees

The villagers of Periyakannanur depend on irrigation tanks for their agriculture and economic survival. The health of the irrigation tanks depends on proper maintenance of the watershed. The vegetation in the watershed helps free flow of water and controls soil erosion. Periyakannanur has a long stretch of barren lands and very limited land under cultivation. The uncultivated land is covered with a variety of thorny bushes, trees and plants. Because of such thick green cover soil erosion is checked.

To prevent soil erosion, the people of Periyakannanur have regulations for the protection of trees within the village boundaries.[108] Two village guards have been appointed for the protection of trees at a nominal salary. The villagers are permitted to collect firewood for personal use from thorny bushes but they are not permitted to cut any tree. They are not permitted to collect fodder from the trees. Collection of fuel for sale is not permitted. The two village guards are responsible for checking any illegal cuttings. The guards can bring any such violation to the notice of the executive committee of the village assembly. Persons violating the rules are fined. The village guards get fifty per cent of the fine amount as an incentive for their work. Sometimes the thorny bushes are harvested by the LCO for some community purpose. Sometimes they are used as a source of income for the community fund.

(g) Participation in Regulation of Grazing

Another important community effort to conserve the green cover in the watershed area is the ban on goat rearing. Goats are considered destroyers of vegetation, agriculture, forest and green cover. Ban on goat rearing is advocated by many environmentalists. Even the

Panchayat Act, 1994 has given the authority to impose restrictions on grazing of goats in the panchayat forest area. But so far, no evidence is available on the use of this power by any panchayat in Tamil Nadu. But the people of Periyakannanur have decided not to rear goats in the village.[109] Because of this ban, the entire village area is covered with thick vegetation. A large number of useful trees are found not only in public lands but also in private lands. The roads and streets of the village are covered by a green canopy. In each house area a few useful trees like neem, tamarind and drumstick trees are found. This could be possible only because of the community's active involvement. In addition, periodical planting of useful trees like neem and tamarind in the common lands is also undertaken in the village.

(h) Participation for the Community Good

The social capital generated by the community organisation can also be used for development purposes. In Periyakannanur village, the LCO could generate people's participation for the community purposes mentioned hereunder.

A building for the local primary school was constructed by the people, contributing labour, material and money. As the teachers in the village school were not sufficient in number, the LCO has agreed to provide the salary for two part time teachers. The part time teachers paid by the village community are helping the regular teachers in handling the classes. Every month the LCO collects Rs. 5 per child from the parents. There are around 150 children studying in the school. Around Rs. 750 is collected from the parents and Rs. 250 is contributed from the village community fund. Two teachers are paid Rs. 500 each as salary. The leaders of the village also work for hundred per cent enrolment of children in the school.[110]

By contributing labour, material and money, a bus stop, a common room and a place of worship have been constructed in the village. The village pond was deepened during 1997 and desilted with the help of the students of a nearby college under their National Service Scheme. Around 100 people worked for two days along with

100 college students for improving the condition of the pond.[111]

The people of the village, through their LCO, have effectively controlled the following social problems : atrocities against the SC people, use of liquor, bootlegging and gambling.

A few years back, when the district administration gave licence for opening a liquor shop in the village, the entire village went to the District Collector's office and, after prolonged agitation, appeal and persuasion, the administration agreed to withdraw the licence.[112]

Like many other villages in Sivagangai district, to ensure a good monsoon, 'community feeding for rain' has become an important event in the village. Each family has to give rice and money as prescribed by the village assembly for the function. The function provides an opportunity to bring people together and share goodwill. The function is a symbol of the solidarity of the community and its concern for the poor and economically weaker sections.[113]

In the Tamil month of Margali, every *kudi* must contribute to the celebration of a month-long programme of morning prayer in the form of money and material. Light refreshments are served after the morning prayer out of the contributions.[114]

(i) Participation in the Management of Community Fund

The community fund of the LCO is operated by the village executive community. In every meeting of the village assembly matters relating to income and expenditure are discussed. After any major expenditure from the fund, details of the expenditure are given in the next meeting. Normally contributors are collected for specific purposes like village festivals, contributions to the village school etc. After the completion of the work, income and expenditure statments are presented in the next village assembly meeting. The village assembly has authorised the executive to spend money to meet emergency demands. Normally such expenditure does not exceed Rs. 300. All major expenditures must have prior sanction from the village assembly.[115]

Savings from the common fund are deposited in the name of three executive committee members jointly in a Cooperative Bank.

Around Rs. 12,000 has accumulated in the account.[116] There is a honorary clerk appointed by the village assembly to maintain the accounts of the community fund. Once a year the income and expenditure statement is presented before the village assembly. Income for the common fund comes from the *kudis* for specific purposes, donations from individuals, income from sale of thorny bushes for fuel from the village common land, savings from village festivals and interest from the investments.

Assurance Provided by LCO

People's participation depends on the assurance given by the institution. The LCO of Periyakannanur is able to give the required assurance to the people on the utility of participation.[117] The most important assurance given by the LCO is on reducing the chances of drop failure. As there is no scope for individual solution to the problem of water scarcity, people have to work collectively to manage the problem. By experience and repeated experiments they have come to an understanding of the role of the community organisation in solving the problems they share together. So the LCO is based on a strongly felt need of the local people. The focus of the LCO is therefore only on protecting the interest of the participants. For several decades the LCO has been able to reduce the risk of crop failure by using a number of locally devised strategies. The LCO has been locally evolved by the stake holders. Even though the Tamil Nadu Peasant Association played a catalyst role in evolving the LCO, the LCO is not a creation of that Association.

The constitution of the LCO is based on local tradition and it is not an externally devised one. The LCO is controlled by the stake holders and there is no external authority to regulate the organisation. The rules and regulations of the organisation are designed by the organisation itself through a participatory process. The organisation is able to do justice to the contributors by assuring reward for their contribution in the form of right to use water and other natural resources. Members are fully assured that non-members cannot enjoy the benefits derived from the collective work of the members.

As discussed in the literature, the boundary of the organisation is properly maintained and non-members are kept out. The relationship between contribution and benefit is fully protected by the organisation. The violators of the rules can be excluded from the organisation. Membership in the organisation requires registration and fulfilment of certain prescribed duties and responsibilities. Trouble makers and free riders can be easily eliminated. The organisation is functioning for more than thirty years with stability. Because the decisions are taken on consensus and there is no process of election and voting, the stability of the organisation is ensured. Most of the rules of the organisations are time tested, traditionally accepted by the community and known to everyone. As the rules are stable and acceptable, smooth enforcement is assured.

The organisation regards the natural resources of the village as common property and ensures that every family gets benefit from them. No individual or no group can encroach upon them or dominate in their use. Even though the land in the tank area is the private property of the individual households, the water in the tank is a common property. Water is distributed among the families as per the rules evolved by the village assembly. At times of water scarcity the water is shared on the principle of equity. Irrespective of the size of the landholding, water in the tank is divided equally among the families. This prevents total failure of the crop, saves at least a portion of the standing crop and guarantees minimum food security to all the families.

Appointment of common irrigators and field guards by the LCO reduces the cost for individual families of irrigating and guarding their individual farm plots. It saves their time and makes them free to attend to some other responsibilities. As many of the families have to attend to different types of farm work and a few of them also earn wages by working in the fields of others, the system of common irrigators is highly cost effective and reduces the burden of individual farmers.

As the LCO of Periyakannanur is not only interested in the availability of water for irrigation but also much concerned about the proper maintenance of the tank, kudimaramathu work is done year after year without any failure. The LCO takes interest not only in the tank but also in the entire watershed area. The ban on goat rearing is imposed in the village with the objective of sustaining the ecology of the village. Because of the appointment of guards, the trees in the common lands are protected from unauthorised wood cutting. The ban on goat rearing is directly responsible for the flourishing of different varieties of trees, bushes and plants in the common and the private lands of the village. Because of the above said regulations soil erosion is controlled and silting of the tank beds is also prevented.

The LCO of Periyakannanur is accountable to its members. Nearly 10 village assembly meetings a year are held to discuss matters relating to the functioning of the LCO. Every aspect of the working of the LCO is frankly debated, particularly matters related to finance and accounts. Even minute details are discussed. The high level of transparency and accountability of the functioning of the organisation encourages participation of the people. The savings account of LCO is jointly operated in a Cooperative Bank in the name of three executive committee members. The accounts are maintained by a honorary accountant. In every meeting the details of the accounts of the LCO's funds are given. The members are assured of the honesty and integrity of the organisation.

Because of the assurance given by the LCO the people of Periyakannanur participate in the process of management of collective goods on voluntary basis and without any outside coercion.

Panchayat and Participation

Periyakannanur Village Panchayat has Periyakannanur as the main village and 10 small hamlets. There are five members in the village panchayat, out of whom two are women and one belongs to Scheduled Caste. The other two are BC men.[118] This village panchayat comes under Kalayarkoil Panchayat Union. The panchayat union ward member representing three village panchayat areas including Periyakannanur Village Panchayat is a male from the backward class.

As per the records available, the panchayats work mainly on

providing services, employment generation and welfare activities for people below poverty line. The village panchayat and the panchayat union have not taken any action regarding irrigation tanks as specified in the Panchayat Act of 1994. Kudimaramathu, compulsory labour of the community for emergency operations, distribution of water and water scarcity management are some of the activities which can be undertaken as per the Act and as per the rules of the panchayat. The village panchayat can also regulate the use of *poramboke* lands, protect the trees in the *poramboke* land, and, impose regulations on grazing and use of fisheries in the water bodies. A careful study of the records and enquiries with the concerned officials have revealed that, in two and half years,[119] no such work has been undertaken in Periyakannanur panchayat in general and Periyakannanur village in particular.

The panchayat President of Periyakannanur village informed the researcher that such activities are mainly done by the LCO and only it can attend to such work. The panchayat President has expressed his inability to mobilise people's participation for the management of natural resources. Instead he says that the panchayat can also support the activities of the LCO. In fact the existence of the LCO helps the panchayats in maintaining certain properties of the panchayat. For example, the panchayat union school has benefited from the LCO through monetary contribution. To harvest the fish in the panchayat union and the village panchayat irrigation tanks and ponds, the LCO pays a nominal fee to organise community fishing in these bodies.

The village panchayat concentrates more on providing services like street lights and water supply. The village panchayat maintains 37 street lights covering a main village and 10 small hamlets. It has 17 sources of water supply, 12 hand pumps, 2 overhead tanks, 2 open wells and one drinking water pond.[120] The panchayat had an income of Rs. 71,201 for the financial year 1997-98.[121] Out of this, Rs. 25,350 was spent on expenditures related to water supply. As per the records available, no money was spent on development of the tank or any other natural resources. The records for the year 1997-98 also reveal that the major source of revenue is the contribution from the State Government. As per the recommendation of the State Finance Commission the village panchayat got Rs. 49,947 and from the share of the land sale registration fees, Rs. 6,789. There is no income from common property resources. The village panchayat has also received Rs. 99,969 for the Jawahar Rozgar Yojana as grant from the State and the Central Government. All this shows that 90 per cent of the income of the panchayat comes from outside agencies. The entire house tax collected for the year is only Rs. 759.35. The President expressed his inability to increase the house tax because of popular resistance.

The Gram Sabha is a device provided by the Act for people's participation in development programmes. But, in Periyakannanur village panchayat, the Gram Sabha does not attract the members to attend.[122] On investigation, it was found that the Gram Sabha meetings were arranged on 2nd October, 1998 and 26th January, 1999, as per the strict orders of the Government. Around Rs. 500 was spent for each meeting on newspaper advertisement, hospitality for the visiting government officials and other expenses. Around 25-30 members attended the meeting.[123] No serious business was conducted except getting signatures. Later signatures were collected from 200 voters to regularise the meeting. As per the records available the Gram Sabha has not discussed any matter relating to people's participation in the management of natural resources so far. The meetings of the village panchayat and the panchayat union also have not discussed any matter related to mobilising people's participation in the management of irrigation tanks and other natural resources available in Periyakannanur village. As per the records and on enquiry it was found that the members of the panchayat union council have not taken any initiative to mobilise people's participation in the management of irrigation tank and other natural resources of Periyakannanur village.[124]

The panchayat President and the members expressed their difficulties in mobilising the people for public work. The panchayat President says that the people feel that, when the panchayat is getting Government funds for its work there is no need for people's contribution. Discussion with an elderly person in the village revealed that people consider the panchayat a government promoted agency to undertake Government Schemes and Programmes. A member of the panchayat said that people wanted to get benefits from the panchayat in the form of aid or loan and did not want to contribute anything back. A former member of the village panchayat told the researcher that the rules of the panchayat related to the management of irrigation tanks and other natural resources were too complex and gave a dominating role to the government officials and little scope for people's participation. According to him, in the name of desilting and maintenance work in the tank, public money could be easily looted by the elected leaders, contractors and government officials. "Works in the tank area are said to be highly remunerative for contractors, elected leaders and government officials," a local school teacher says.

In a group discussion, the farmers of the village, brought to the notice of the researcher a significant deficiency of the village panchayat and the panchayat union. Periyakannanur panchayat covers 11 hamlets and the panchayat may find it difficult to take care of local natural resources in such a vast area and only village-specific organisations can ensure people's participation in natural resources management. A farmer asked, "what can the panchayat union council do for the local natural resources? The panchayat union office is located 30 km away from the village. I have never seen the panchayat union council member for the area who is a businessman in Sivagangai Town. What does he know about our irrigation tank? After all, he hails from some other village. By handing over our village tank to the panchayat union, the State has encroached upon an important local wealth".

Process of Accommodating the LCO

As per the government records the LCO does not exist. Wade and Sen Gupta have also found in their studies the similar status of community organisation in government records. Most LCOs do not want to record their functioning with government agencies, because they use some of the natural resources owned by the panchayat or the Government, which may legally constitute an offence. In view to this, the LCO is not a registered organisation.

The elected leaders of the village panchayat and the panchayat union council know every detail of the LCO's role in managing irrigation tanks and other natural resources.[125] In Periyakannanur Village, the President does not question the role of the LCO in managing common property resources. Instead he tries to accommodate the LCO to the maximum possible extent.

The LCO protects the trees in the common land of the village. The very presence of a strong LCO has kept poachers away from the boundaries of the village. The President of the village panchayat said that, in the absence of the LCO, within a month or two the entire vegetation in the village area may vanish and that the village panchayat has no machinery to protect it.

During floods, the village panchayat cannot protect the tank structure as required by the Panchayat Act and it expects the LCO to mobilise the local people for such emergency operations. In Periyakannanur village the President of the village panchayat does not consider the LCO a rival organisation. Instead he prefers to work along with the LCO.[126]

NOTES

1. District Rural Development Agency, *District Profile*, Sivạgangai: District Rural Development Agency, 1998, p. 6.
2. *Ibid.*
3. *Ibid.*
4. District Collector Office, *District Resource Survey Profile*, Sivagangai: Collector Office, 1997, pp. 15-16.
5. *Ibid.*, p. 19.
6. *Ibid.*, p. 20.
7. *Ibid.*
8. *Ibid.*
9. *Ibid.*
10. *Ibid.*, p. 22.
11. *Ibid.*
12. *Ibid.*, pp. 59-60.
13. *Ibid.*, pp. 19-20.

14. Cited in K. Palanisamy, R. Balasubramanian and A. Mohamed Ali, *Present Status and Future Strategies of Tank Irrigation in Tamil Nadu*, Coimbatore: Tamil Nadu Agricultural University, 1997, p. 33.
15. *Ibid.*
16. *Ibid.*
17. *Ibid.*
18. Block Panchayat Office, *Kalayar Kovil Block Profile*, Kalayar Kovil: Block Panchayat Office, 1998.
19. *Ibid.*
20. *Ibid.*
21. V. Rengarasan, *Thirukanapper (Tamil)*, Sivagangai: Gnana Peedam, 1998, Annexure-10.
22. *Ibid.*
23. M. Monoharan, *Maruthirupandia Mannargal (Tamil)*, Sivagangai: Annam Publishers, 1994, p. 596.
24. *Ibid.*, pp. 551-561.
25. *Ibid.*, pp. 353-358.
26. Nirmal Sen Gupta, *Managing Common Property: Irrigation in India and Philippines*, New Delhi: Sage Publications, 1991, p. 77.
27. Interview with the President, LCO, Soosaipattinam village, Kalayar Kovil Block, Sivagangai District, May 1998.
28. Interview with the President, LCO, Pulikanmai, May 1998.
29. LCO, *Kudi Register*, Pulikanmai: Village, 1998.
30. Details are engraved in the tank sluices, Pulikanmai Irrigation Tank, Field Study, May 1998.
31. LCO, *Kudi Register*, *Op.cit.*
32. Interview with the President, LCO, Pulikanmai, May 1998.
33. Information provided by Panchayat Clerk, Pulikanmai, May 1998.
34. Interview with the President, LCO, Pulikanmai, June 1998.
35. LCO, *Kudi Register*, Pulikanmai: LCO, 1998.
36. Information provided by Panchayat Clerk, Pulikanmai, May 1990.
37. LCO, *Op.cit.*
38. *Ibid.*
39. Information provided by President LCO, Pulikanmai, May 1998.
40. *Ibid.*
41. *Ibid.*
42. *Ibid.*
43. *Ibid.*
44. LCO, *Pulikanmai LCO Accounts Book 1977*, Pulikanmai: LCO, 1977.
45. Interview with the President, LCO, Pulikanmai, May 1998.
46. *Ibid.*
47. *Ibid.*
48. *Ibid.*
49. *Ibid.*

50. *Ibid.*
51. *Ibid.*
52. *Ibid.*
53. *Ibid.*
54. Interview with the Members of the SC households of Pulikanmai Village, May 1998.
55. Group discussion with the Members of Executive Committee, LCO, June 1998.
56. *Ibid.*
57. *Ibid.*
58. Information provided by President LCO, Pulikanmai, June 1998.
59. *Ibid.*
60. *Ibid.*
61. *Ibid.*
62. *Ibid.*
63. Group discussion with members of the Village Assembly LCO, Pulikanmai, May 1998.
64. *Ibid.*
65. *Ibid.*
66. *Ibid.*
67. *Ibid.*
68. LCO, *Pulikanmai LCO Accounts Book 1996-97*, Pulikanmai: LCO, 1997.
69. R. Wade, *Village Republic: Economic Conditions for Collective Action in South India*, Bombay: Orient Longman, 1987, p. 211.
70. LCO, *Op.cit.*, 1997.
71. *Ibid.*
72. *Ibid.*
73. Interview with President, LCO, Pulikanmai, 1996-97.
74. LCO, *Op.cit.*, 1996-97.
75. LCO, *Pulikanmai LCO Accounts Book 1998-89*, Pulikanmai: LCO, 1989.
76. LCO, *Op.cit.*, 1997.
77. *Ibid.*
78. Villae Panchayat Office, *Paruthikanmai Village Panchayat Quarterly Report*, Paruthikanmai: Village Panchayat, December 1997.
79. Block Panchayat Office, *Local Irrigation Tank Register*, Kalayar Kovil: Block Panchayat Office, 1998.
80. Interview with President, Paruthikanmai Village Panchayat, December 1998.
81. Village Panchayat, *Paruthikanmai Village Panchayat Income and Expenditure Statement 1996-97 and 1997-98*, Paruthikanmai: Village Panchayat, 1998.
82. *Ibid.*
83. *Ibid.*
84. *Ibid.*

85. Village Panchayat, *Minutes of the Paruthikanmai Village Panchayat Meetings 1996-97,* Paruthikanmai: Village Panchayat, 1997.
86. *Ibid.*
87. Village Panchayat, *Op.cit.*, 1996-97 and 97-98.
88. Interview with President, Village Panchayat, Paruthikanmai, December 1998.
89. Village Panchayat, *Periyakannanur Village Panchayat Quarterly Report*, Periyakannanur: Village Panchayat, March 1998.
90. Information provided by the Village Panchayat Clerk, Periyakannanur.
91. LCO, *Kudi Register*, Periyakannanur: LCO, 1998.
92. Information provided by the President, LCO, Periyakannanur, May 1998.
93. *Ibid.*
94. *Ibid.*
95. Group discussion with the Members of SC households, Periyakannanur Village, June 1998.
96. LCO, *Kudi Register*, Periyakannanur: Village, 1998.
97. *Ibid.*
98. Interview with President, LCO, Periyakannanur, May 1998.
99. *Ibid.*
100. Group discussion with the Members of the Village Assembly, May 1998.
101. *Ibid.*
102. Group discussion with the Executive Committee Members of LCO, Periyakannanur, May 1998.
103. *Ibid.*
104. *Ibid.*
105. *Ibid.*
106. *Ibid.*
107. *Ibid.*
108. Interview with President, LCO, Periyakannanur, May 1998.
109. *Ibid.*
110. *Ibid.*
111. *Ibid.*
112. *Ibid.*
113. *Ibid.*
114. *Ibid.*
115. Group discussion with the Members of the Executive Committee, Periyakannanur, May 1998.
116. *Ibid.*
117. *Ibid.*
118. Village Panchayat, *Periyakannanur Village Panchayat Quarterly Report,* Periyakannanur: Village Panchayat, December 1996.
119. Interview with President, Periyakannanur Village Panchayat, December 1998.
120. Village Panchayat, *Periyakannanur Village Panchayat Quarterly Report*, Periyakannanur: Village Panchayat, December 1998.

121. Village Panchayat, *Periyakannanur Village Panchayat Income and Expenditure Statment 1997-98*, Periyakannanur: Village Panchayat, 1998.
122. Interview with President, Pulikanmai Village Panchayat, January 1999.
123. *Ibid.*
124. Information provided by the Extension Officer (Panchayat), Kalayar Kovil Panchayat Union, December 1998.
125. *Ibid.*
126. Interview with President, Periyakannanur Village Panahcyat, January 1999.

4

CHOICE OF THE COMMUNITY

The study of natural resource management by the community requires "a close feel of the field and knowledge of the local oral history and current situation of the area,"[1] according to Jodha, who has done one of the most important studies on common property resources in India. He advocates a mixture of the methods of anthropology and social sciences. To him, using rigorous statistical methods may rupture the beauty of insights and understanding conveyed by descriptive accounts of the community institution's role in the management of scarce natural resources. He recommends participatory observation, collection of oral histories, group discussions and case histories as efficient methods of understanding the issues in such type of studies.[2] In recent times Participatory Rural Appraisal (PRA) is used by scholars as a reliable method of research in some specific areas of study like community involvement in local natural resources. Against this background Jodha recommends analysis of data collected by a structured schedule by a simple method involving bivariate tables.[3] He says, "the relative simplicity and transparency associated with this method of information processing prove to be one of the main reasons for appeal and utility/usability"[4] of the study. Against this background this study has presented data collected by a structured schedule from the representatives of the households in a simple form of tables with the percentages calculated and the same have been explained through descriptive analysis.

The data collected have been analysed under the following headings :

1. Profile of the Respondents
2. Assurance
3. Participation
4. Discussion on Hypotheses.

Profile of the Respondents

Scholars like Wade and Oakerson maintain that the socio-economic and ecological setting of the people play a crucial role in their participation in natural resources management. Wade maintains that the survival need of the people facilities development of organisations for collective management of common natural resources.[5] Oakerson also regards ecological setting as a determining variable in collective action for the management of common resources.[6] Wade argues that the landholding pattern plays a key role in determining the long enduring participation of the people.[7] Studies in West Bengal have found that land reform and participatory local governance have significant relationship.[8] Against this background, the study of the respondents' socio-economic setting has also to be presented here. Only a few data which are considered vital and helpful for analysing the research problem are discussed here.

TABLE 4.1: Age-wise Distribution of the Respondents

Sl.No.	*Category*	*Pulikanmai*	*Periyakannanur*
1.	Below 25	3 (7.50)	5 (8.19)
2.	26-40	10 (25.00)	14 (22.95)
3.	41-50	12 (30.00)	22 (36.06)
4.	51-60	11 (27.50)	15 (24.59)
5.	61-70	4 (10.00)	5 (8.19)

Source: Computed.

Note : Figures in parentheses indicate the percentage and those outside the parentheses indicate the number of respondents in all the tables in this Chapter.

According to Table 4.1, which presents the age-wise distribution of the respondents, most of the respondents are between the ages of forty to sixty. As the oldest males represent the households in the village assembly meetings, the researcher tried to contact them. In a few cases young people were also contacted depending on availability and interest. Generally, in LCOs, the heads of the households influence the decision-making process. Their experience and knowledge are valuable to the LCOs.

TABLE 4.2: Sex-wise Distribution of the Respondents

Sl. No.	*Category*	*Pulikanmai*	*Periyakannanur*
1.	Male	36 (90.00)	56 (91.80)
2.	Female	4 (10.00)	5 (8.19)

Source: Computed.

As per Table 4.2, which shows the sex-wise distribution of the respondents, most of the respondents from the two villages are males. In the Indian rural paradigm, gender bias in favour of men is a fact. In the study villages also the oldest males represent the households in the village assembly meetings. Females also show interest and observe the proceedings of the meetings. But, in the decision-making process, the males dominate. It does not mean that women are ill-treated in the villages. Women can move freely in the fields day and night without any fear in the study area. In one case the LCO in Pulikanmai ex-communicated a family for ill-treating the doughter-in-law on dowry grounds. There is a saying in Periyakannanur, "Even a destitute woman can live in Kannanur (Periyakannanur) with honour."

TABLE 4.3: Community-wise Distribution of the Respondents

Sl. No.	*Category*	*Pulikanmai*	*Periyakannanur*
1.	SC	10 (25.00)	18 (29.50)
2.	BC	30 (75.00)	43 (70.50)
3.	FC	—	—

Source: Computed.

The community-wise distribution of the respondents is presented in Table 4.3, according to which, SC respondents are in significant number. Population-wise, the SC is the second largest caste group in the study area. In Periyakannanur all the SC families have irrigated land. There is no caste discrimination in the functioning of the LCO. In this village the status of the SC people is better than that in other parts of Tamil Nadu.

In Pulikanmai, due to Christian missionary activities, the intensity of the practice of untouchability is reduced. The SC families and Christian udayar families could came to an electoral understanding in the 1996 village panchayat election. As a result, the candidate sponsored by the LCO was elected President of the village panchayat. In return, the LCO supported an SC female candidate's candidacy from a general ward of the village panchayat and the candidate was elected.

TABLE 4.4: Religion-wise Distribution of the Respondents

Sl. No.	*Category*	*Pulikanmai*	*Periyakannanur*
1.	Hindu	12 (30.00)	57 (93.44)
2.	Christians	27 (70.00)	—
3.	Muslims	—	4 (6.55)

Source : Computed.

Table 4.4 presents the religion-wise distribution of the respondents. According to it, most of the respondents in Pulikanmai are Christians. They also belong to a single caste. Most of the Hindus belong to the SC. This makes for social cohesion in the village. In Periyakannanur most of the respondents are Hindus. There are 4 Muslim respondents and no Christian ones. In both the villages perfect religious harmony is maintained. The religious diversity of the study villages does not hinder the process of collective action for the maintenance of common property resources.

As per Table 4.5, which shows the occupation-wise distribution of the respondents, most of the respondents from both the study villages have agriculture and agriculture related occupations as their

TABLE 4.5: Occupation-wise Distribution of the Respondents

Sl. No.	*Category*	*Pulikanmai*	*Periyakannanur*
1.	Agriculture	24 (60.00)	50 (81.96)
2.	Agricultural Employment	12 (30.00)	8 (13.11)
3.	Business	2 (5.00)	2 (3.27)
4.	Government/Organised	2 (5.00)	1 (1.63)
5.	Unorganised industries	—	—

Source: Computed.

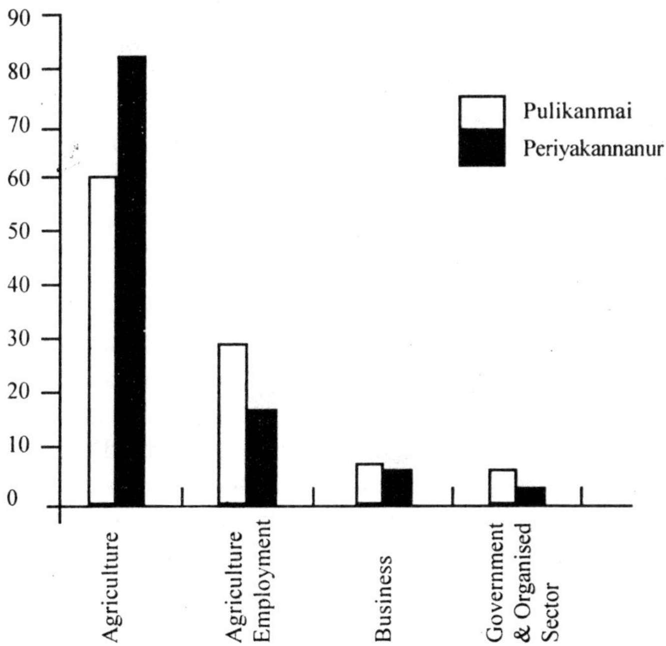

Source: Computed.

Fig. 4.1 : Occupation-wise Distribution of Respondents.

main occupation. As tanks are the primary source of irrigation, agriculture in the villages depends on the proper management of the irrigation tanks. As the study area is industrially backward, the scope for alternative employment is very limited. In this context the people of the study area regard irrigation tanks as valuable resources. The people's interest in these resources is intact. In urban settings the tanks are neglected because of the economic status of the residents of the area. Land is integrated into the process of marketisation. Because of the commercial value of the land, people do not give importance to the irrigation value of the tanks. So scholars like Wade consider that the remotedness of the resources from urban centres plays a role in people's interest in conserving the resources.

TABLE 4.6: Landholding-wise Distribution of the Respondents

Sl. No.	*Category*	*Pulikanmai*	*Periyakannanur*
1.	Landless	8 (20.00)	—
2.	Upto one acre	10 (25.00)	19 (31.14)
3.	Above 1 acre to 2.5 acres	16 (40.00)	34 (55.73)
4.	Above 2.5 acres to 5 acres	4 (10.00)	6 (9.83)
5.	Above 5 acres	2 (5.00)	2 (3.27)

Source: Computed.

The landholding-wise distribution of the respondents is presented in Table 4.6, according to which, in both the villages of the study, the researcher could not find any dominating group of landlords. The presence of such a dominating group may destabilise the process of collective action. But, in the study villages, the land distribution pattern is favourable for participation of most of the respondents in tank management. In Periyakannanur village, since the land is distributed among all the households, the participation of the marginalised sections like the Scheduled Caste is assured. This has resulted in the improvement of the social status of the SC people in the village. The experiments of West Bengal in land reform and participatory development process help us to understand the situation in Periyakannanur village.[9] In Pulikanmai also, the land distribution and participation in community effort have a relationship. The landholding SC people are accepted into the participatory management system.

Assurance

Scholars like Wade[10] and Platteau[11] explain the role of institutions as providers of assurance to individuals on the behaviour of other individuals in the process of collective action for common good. In the process of collective action every individual wants to be assured about the behaviour of the other individuals and he does not want to be exploited by the others in the process of participation. He wants some institutional arrangement to regulate and coordinate the behaviour of every one in the process. The literature on natural resource management gives a prominent role to institutions in the process of collective action as providers of assurance to the participants. For this study assurance has the following components:

1. Capacity to protect the interest of the participants
2. Maintenance of boundary
3. Participants' control
4. Autonomy
5. Efficiency
6. Stability
7. Adaptability
8. Sustainability
9. Equity
10. Transparency and Accountability.

Success in ensuring people's participation for natural resource management depends on the institution's ability to assure the participants of its capacity to protect the participants' interests.

Assurance by Panchayats

Table 4.7 presents the assurance by the panchayats on the protection of the participants' interests. In the study villages, people critically depend on the irrigation tanks for their survival because of topographical and economic reasons. As in Kotapalle village studied by Wade, here also the interests of the participants are significantly

TABLE 4.7: Assurance by Panchayats on Protection of Interests

Sl. No.	*Name of the Village*	*Protection of Interests*		
		Fully Assured	*Fairly Assured*	*Not Assured*
1.	Pulikanmai	—	2 (5.00)	38 (95.00)
2.	Periyakannanur	—	—	61 (100.00)

Source: Computed.

affected by water scarcity and risk of crop failure.[12]

The above table 4.7 shows that a vast majority of the respondents do not believe that the panchayats can protect their interests in the irrigation tank and other natural resources. The panchayat cannot solve the problem of water scarcity and protect them from crop failure by supplying water for irrigation. As Vani has pointed out, tank management is not a priority for the panchayats. As Jodha points out, "Panchayati Raj Insitutions despite the recent focus on genuine interest in decentralisation, may not be substitute for local organisation of stake holders as the goals of the panchayats are too diversified and natural resources contribute a small component."[13] Because of the electrocal process, state control and bureaucratization, the panchayats are not able to protect the interests of the real participants. "In the name of tank maintenance social forestry and soil conservation the panchayats facilitate misappropriation of public money," a retired official of the Panchayati Raj Department said to the researcher. Jodha also agrees with this view and says that, in the name of natural resource management, the panchayats want to get more and more money from the government.[14]

The assurance given by the panchayats on maintenance of boundary is shown in Table 4.8. In the literature on natural resource management, maintenance of boundary is considered the most significant assurance required by the participants from the institution. Boundary here means the restriction by the institution of benefits from the natural resources to the participants who contribute to the maintenance and development of the resources. If the

TABLE 4.8: Assurance by Panchayats on Maintenance of Boundary

Sl. No.	*Name of the Village*	*Maintenance of Boundary*		
		Fully Assured	*Fairly Assured*	*Not Assured*
1.	Pulikanmai	—	—	40 (100.00)
2.	Periyakannanur	—	—	61 (100.00)

Source: Computed.

institution fails to do this, the interest in participation will decline. All the respondents are not sure about the panchayats' ability to restrict the benefits to the contributors. A scholar argues that the panchayats convert natural resources into "open access resourcess".[15] If they are 'opened' to unrestricted use it will result in the tragedy of commons. Because of the inability of the panchayats, many tank areas in Tamil Nadu are under illegal encroachment.[16] Trees in the tank area and in *poramboke* lands are cut by poachers. The panchayats are not able to protect valuable resources like trees, fisheries and minerals like gravel and sand. Hundreds of lorry loads of sand are taken away from the panchayat areas by contractors after giving bribes to revenue officials and panchayat Presidents. This is a great threat to the environment of the villages.[17] In Periyakannanur and Pulikanmai people do not have faith in the panchayat's ability to deny the use of resources to non-contributors, non-members and non-participants. So the vast majority of the respondents do not think that the panchayats have the ability to protect the natural resources from encroachment. They do not think that the panchayats can take the responsibility of regulating water use and prevent illegal use of it.

Table 4.9 presents the assurance given by the panchayats on participants' control. Most of the development programmes have the approach of "I govern, you participate." The Panchayat Act and the rules provide for kudimaramathu. But, as per the Act, the entire process of kudimaramathu and other tank maintenance work are controlled by the District Collector, the Revenue Department and the Union Engineer. Ostrom explains the need for stake holders' control over the organisation of common property resources.[18] Only they can

TABLE 4.9: Assurance by Panchayats on Participants' Control

Sl. No.	*Name of the Village*	*Participant's Control*		
		Fully Assured	*Fairly Assured*	*Not Assured*
1.	Pulikanmai	—	2 (5.00)	38 (95.00)
2.	Periyakannanur	—	3 (4.91)	58 (95.08)

Source: Computed.

evolve rules to suit their needs and only they can enforce the rules. As the panchayats do not allow the people who are the stake holders to take important decisions, the people are not ready to work along with the panchayats on a long-term basis. A vast majority of the respondents in both the study villages do not regard the panchayats as institutions controlled by them in the context of natural resources management. A former member of the village panchayat explained how the tank maintenance was dominated by the Union Engineer and the Public Works Department and how even the panchayat union council could not take any decision on the tanks. In both the study villages most of the responents did not feel that they had any control over the process of management in the panchayats. They could only give petitions and memorandums to the officials on issues related to the tanks. In group discussions with the village panchayat Presidents it was found that they believe that the Panchayati Raj Institutions are fully controlled by Government officials.

TABLE 4.10: Assurance by Panchayats on Autonomy

Sl. No.	*Name of the Village*	*Autonomous Status*		
		Fully Assured	*Fairly Assured*	*Not Assured*
1.	Pulikanmai	—	—	40 (100.00)
2.	Periyakannanur	—	—	61 (100.00)

Source: Computed.

The assurance given by the panchayats on autonomy is

presented in Table 4.10. Ostrom maintains, "The right of users to devise their own institutions must not be challenged by external governmental authorities." He regards this right as a design principle for a long enduring self-governing system which can ensure people's participation.[19] The need for real self-governance is insisted upon here. Highly centralised institutions may not be responsive to the needs of the people and cannot work effectively as participatory institutions. Too much of government control will destroy the participatory component of local institutions.[20] A close study of the rules of the Tamil Nadu Panchayat Act, 1994 reveals the dominant role of various departments of the State in the process of natural resources management. Revenue, Forest, Public Works, Rural Development and Fisheries are the departments involved in the process. The District Collector has the ultimate power of decision-making in respect of the village panchayats. Any natural resource under the panchayats can be taken back by the Government. As per Section 121 of the Tamil Nadu Panchayat Act, the unreserved forests vested in village panchayats can be taken back by the Government and the compensation is fixed by the State, which cannot be challenged in any Court of law by the concerned panchayat.

None of the respondents in both the study villages, according to the table, regard the panchayats as autonomous. Scholars like Palanithurai agree with such a view.[21] This status of the panchayats affects people's participation in the acitivities related to natural resources management. In many villages of Tamil Nadu the panchayats are helplessly watching the looting of their natural resources against their will. Millions of rupees worth of minor minerals are looted from the panchayat areas.[22] Normally the revenue authorities undermine the role of the panchayats in conserving natural resources, which are looted by outsiders with the help of government officials and politicians.[23]

Table 4.11 presents the assurance given by the panchayats on equity. If an organisation gives assurance of fairness and equity in its transactions, it can command respect from its members. Unless an organisation has an image of fair treatment of all its members, there can be no sustainable participation.[24] Most of the respondents of both

TABLE 4.11: Assurance by Panchayats on Equity

Sl. No.	Name of the Village	Equity		
		Fully Assured	Fairly Assured	Not Assured
1.	Pulikanmai	—	2 (5.00)	38 (95.00)
2.	Periyakannanur	—	4 (6.55)	57 (93.44)

Source: Computed.

the study villages do not feel that Panchayati Raj Institutions give any such assurance. Some scholars believe that, in Tamil Nadu, in the panchayats, wealthy or powerful people are able to obtain the right to exploit common property resources at very low rates in auctions.[25] A respondent told the researcher that only powerful and influential people can get benefits from the panchayats. In the study villages there is no dominance by the landed aristocracy and the people are used to a culture of equity. Even small benefits from Common Property Resources like fisheries are distributed equally among all the families and no one can get an extra share without sufficient reason.

In the distribution of welfare schemes, the Panchayati Raj Institutions have earned a very bad reputation and the panchahats have become a source of corruption in rural areas.[26] In this context people in Periyakannanur and Pulikanmai, according to the table, are not confident of the Panchayati Raj Institutions' ability to be fair and equitable in the distribution of benefits from the natural resources. In the distribution of tank water for irrigation, particularly in times of water scarcity, institutions must have a reputation for fairness and equity. The respondents do not think that the panchayats have such a reputation.

The assurance given by the panchayats on efficiency is presented in Table 4.12. Efficiency in the management of the water in the tank affects the economic survival of the people in Pulikanmai and Periyakannanur villages. As the rains are scarce, seasonal, and, sporadic, the rain water has to be properly collected. For this the supply channels must be kept clean to allow free flow of the rain

TABLE 4.12: Assurance by Panchayats on Efficiency

Sl. No.	*Name of the Village*	*Efficiency*		
		Fully Assured	*Fairly Assured*	*Not Assured*
1.	Pulikanmai	—	2 (5.00)	38 (95.00)
2.	Periyakannanur	—	—	61 (100.00)

Source: Computed.

water to the tank. The harvested water has to be carefully distributed to benefit the maximum area. Water scarcity has to be managed by imposing regulations acceptable to all. Scholars like Oakerson regard the efficiency of the institution as one of the most important determinants of participation.[27] Unless efficiency is ensured, the participants may not contribute to the organisation. The decision-making process must be responsive to the immediate and the long standing requirements of the participants. The cost of the institutional operation must be acceptable to the participants. Most of the respondents in both the study villages, according to the table, do not regard the Panchayati Raj Institutions as efficient enough to manage the irrigation tanks. One of the respondents told the researcher that the panchayats were not able to maintain even hand pumps and street lights properly. People would be very happy if the panchayats could carry out such activities properly. School buildings of the panchayat unions are not properly maintained in spite of repeated requests from the villagers of Periyakannanur. Against this background the villagers do not have confidence in the panchayats' ability to manage natural resources. A farmer in Periyakannanur said that he could not even think of the management of the local irrigation tank, the distribution of the water and the sharing of scarce water by the panchayat union.

Table 4.13 shows the assurance given by the panchayats on stability. Irrigation tanks in Tamil Nadu have been developed through hundreds of years of community effort. These tanks were maintained by local communities generation after generation. Stable local institutions are required to manage these tanks with people's participation. Conventions, customs and traditions play a significant

TABLE 4.13: Assurance by Panchayats on Stability

Sl. No.	*Name of the Village*	*Stability*		
		Fully Assured	*Fairly Assured*	*Not Assured*
1.	Pulikanmai	—	4 (10.00)	36 (90.00)
2.	Periyakannanur	—	—	61 (100.00)

Source: Computed.

role in giving stability to the system of management by LCOs. Unstable institutions cannot manage fragile natural resources like forests and irrigation tanks. The Panchayati Raj Institutions do not offer such stability. One reason is the historical problem related to the panchayats. Panchayat laws have been changed at least four times after Independence in Tamil Nadu. Many of the functions given to the panchayats by the Act of 1958 have been eroded and the Act of 1994 has not restored them. In many aspects the Act of 1994 is regarded as a setback to the Panchayati Raj System in Tamil Nadu.[28]

Jodha feels that the electoral process destabilises Panchayati Raj Institutions.[29] Pant feels that, in panchayats, because of the political process, factionalism has become a major threat to the institutional stability.[30] When the institutions are not stable, they cannot predict the outcome to the people.

Most of the respondents in both the study villages, according to the table, do not think that the Panchayati Raj Institutions are stable enough to ensure participation in a sustainable manner. Irregular elections to the panchayats and frequent change of Acts and rules are the major destabilising factors. Electoral competition, political factions, rivalry between different hamlets within the same village panchayat, and, intervention by government officials contribute to institutional instability, which has a deterrent effect on voluntary cooperation among the participants for common good.

The assurance given by the panchayats on adaptability is shown in Table 4.14. Institutions managing natural resources must have the capacity of adaptability to the changing situations. Ostrom regards

TABLE 4.14: Assurance by Panchayats on Adaptability

Sl. No.	Name of the Village	Adaptability		
		Fully Assured	Fairly Assured	Not Assured
1.	Pulikanmai	—	5 (12.50)	37 (87.50)
2.	Periyakannanur	—	9 (14.75)	52 (85.24)

Source: Computed.

adaptability as one of the most important criteria for evaluating an institution's capacity to manage natural resources.[31] Keeping this in mind, Ostrom feels that decisions on operational rules must be taken locally, by the users of the resources, according to the needs of the context.[32] The rules of the panchayats relating to natural resource management are based on the colonial policies of the British administration. Particularly, Section 133 of the Tamil Nadu Panchayat Act, 1994 has its roots in the Compulsory Labour Act of 1858 and the Madras Panchayat Act of 1920. Both these Acts centralised the management of resources under rigid state control and the rigidity established by the colonial administration has not been removed even after fifty years of Independence.[33] As the Government is still influenced by the policies framed nearly 150 years ago, local decision-making is still a distant dream. The rigid control of the State over the resources vested with the panchayats does not allow operational flexibility at the local level to facilitate people's participation. Most of the respondents from both the study villages, as per the table, do not think that the Panchayati Raj Institutions are capable of adapting to the changing situations to facilitate better participation of the people. Field level decisions are required for the efficient management of the resources according to the needs of the local situations. People do not think that the panchayats have such operational freedom to take decisions to fulfil the expectations of the people.

Table 4.15 presents the assurance given by the panchayats on sustainability. Most of the respondents from both the study villages, according to the table, do not think that the Panchayati Raj

TABLE 4.15: Assurance by Panchayats on Sustainability

Sl. No.	Name of the Village	Sustainability		
		Fully Assured	Fairly Assured	Not Assured
1.	Pulikanmai	2 (5.00)	3 (7.50)	35 (87.50)
2.	Periyakannanur	3 (4.91)	5 (8.19)	53 (86.88)

Source: Computed.

Institutions have the ability to maintain and develop the irrigation tanks and the other natural resources in a sustainable manner. Irrigation systems have been sustained by local communities for hundreds of years through a process of community participation. Development of trees in the village common lands has also required several decades of effort. Periyakannanur and Pulikanmai have a number of fifty-to-hundred-year-old trees, protected by the community. But most of the programmes of the panchayats like social forestry and fisheries development have income generation as the primary objective. As the tenure of an elected panchayat is only five years, the elected leaders also do not have any long-term interest in conserving trees and irrigation tanks.[34] In contrast, they are interested in cutting trees for some short-term gains to generate funds for popular schemes like purchase of colour television sets and construction of shelters at the village bus stops. One of the respondents told the researcher that only because of the presence of a strong LCO, hundreds of trees in the village common lands have been preserved. In the absence of the LCO, the officials of the panchayat and the Revenue Department might have cut them and sold them years back.

The assurance given by the panchayats on transparency and accountability is presented in Table 4.16. Accountability and transparency are two important factors in the study of collective action. Free flow of information builds mutual assurance of cooperation and the fear of defection is eliminated. In the case of absence of transparency, chances for defection are very high in collective action.

TABLE 4.16: Assurance by Panchayats on Transparency and Accountability

Sl. No.	*Name of the Village*	*Transparency and Accountability*		
		Fully Assured	*Fairly Assured*	*Not Assured*
1.	Pulikanmai	—	—	40 (100.00)
2.	Periyakannanur	—	—	61 (100.00)

Source: Computed.

The Gram Sabha has been introduced to ensure transparency and accountability in Panchayati Raj Institutions. But it has not been fully operationalised.[35] Even if it is operationalised, it does not cover the functioning of the panchayat union, which holds a lion's share of the powers and functions. Many of the natural resources come under its authority and the local people have no means of ensuring transparency and accountability in the functioning of the panchayat union. Even the village panchayat Presidents do not know how the money earned from the social forestry produce in their village tanks is spent.[36] People do not know how the money is spent by the members of the panchayat union council of their area and by the panchayat union on works relating to irrigation tanks.[37] None of the respondents, as per the table, thinks that the panchayats practise accountability and transparency. Because of this deficiency, the people are not willing to contribute labour and money to the panchayats on works like kudimaramathu or for the development of forestry in the village.

Assurance by LCOs

Table 4.17 presents the assurance given by the LCOs on the protection of the participants' interests. Sustainable participation is only possible if the participants' interests are assured by the institution which facilitates participation.[38] Most of the respondents from the two study villages, according to the table, believe that their interests in the irrigation tanks and other natural resources are well protected by the LCOs. Without these institutions, agriculture, on

TABLE 4.17: Assurance by Panchayats on Protection of Interests

Sl. No.	*Name of the Village*	*Protection of Interests*		
		Fully Assured	*Fairly Assured*	*Not Assured*
1.	Pulikanmai	34 (85.00)	5 (12.50)	1 (2.50)
2.	Periyakannanur	56 (91.80)	5 (8.19)	—

Source: Computed.

which the villagers depend, cannot survive. The villages are located in an industrially backward area and so other employment opportunities are very scarce. There is very limited scope for rainfed farming. The rains are seasonal, irregular and sporadic and the soil does not retain moisture for long periods. Groundwater availability is limited and the available groundwater is saline. Because of these reasons the irrigation tanks have become the most important assets of the villages. Wade, in his study at Kotapalle village in Andhra Pradesh, found a similar situation where the risk and the scarcity associated with irrigation have created institutions for protecting the interests of the people.[39] In Pulikanmai and Periyakannanur also the LCOs have the prime objective of saving the farmers from the risk of crop loss due to water scarcity. Discussions with the local villagers reveal that, but for the functioning of the LCO, they cannot get a good harvest. For generations the LCOs have protected the people from crop loss. Not only in the management of the irrigation tank, but also in other areas like the protection of the watershed by conserving the green cover and regulating grazing, the LCOs protect the interests of the people. Even minor resources like fisheries in the water bodies are protected and properly distributed by the LCOs. In other areas like noon meal centre and village school, the people's interests are protected by the LCOs.

Panchayati Raj Institutions regard the natural resources as sources of revenue for the panchayats. Studies in Tamil Nadu show that the social forestry in the irrigation tanks has not benefited the farmers who depend on it.[40] A study in Madhya Pradesh also has found that, in village panchayats, the benefits from the social forestry scheme have not benefited the people in the neighbourhood.[41] Discussions with the villagers of the study area elicited their opinion that the Panchayati Raj Institutions mostly serve the interests of the elected leaders, the government officials and the contractors. Jodha also has found that the natural resources are exploited by the rich and powerful with the help of the Panchayati Raj Institutions and that they do not serve the intersts of the needy people.[42]

TABLE 4.18: Assurance by LCOs on Maintenance of Boundary

Sl. No.	*Name of the Village*	*Maintenance of Boundary*		
		Fully Assured	*Fairly Assured*	*Not Assured*
1.	Pulikanmai	38 (95.00)	2 (5.00)	—
2.	Periyakannanur	56 (91.80)	5 (8.19)	—

Source: Computed.

The assurance given by LCOs on the maintenance of boundary is presented in Table 4.18. Ostrom finds that clear boundaries, defining participants, are required for the proper management of common resources by the participants.[43] The institutions must define who can control the resources, how they can use the resources, and how they can share the benefits. Most of the respondents from both the study villages, as per the table, say that the LCOs maintain boundary to their satisfaction. The community organisations in Pulikanmai and Periyakannanur have a system of enrolment of members who can participate in the management of local natural resources. Residence in the village, ownership of land in the village and having one's name in the voters' list are not sufficient to become a member in the LCO. They have to enroll their name by registering with the LCO. By registering their name they obtain the right to participate in the activities of the LCO. Only members can participate in the affairs of the LCO. Members have to fulfil certain obligations before getting any benefit out of collective action. Key decisions are made only by the members and membership gives them identity with the community.

In both the study villages institutions are strong enough to exclude non-contributors from enjoying the benfits. Even attendance in village assembly meeting is compulsory. Without proper reason no family can avoid attending the village assembly meeting. One cannot take water from the tank against the rules of the LCO. No outsider can cut a tree within the boundary of the village and get away with it. No one can graze a goat in the common lands of the village. In the management of natural resources both villages have maintained boundary to the satisfaction of the respondents. Once boundary is opened, the resources become open access resources, meaning that anyone can use the resources without any restriction and without fulfilling any obligation. The panchayats are not capable of strictly enforcing the boundaries and, therefore, in many parts of India, resources owned by them have become open access resources.

TABLE 4.19: Assurance by LCOs on Participant's Control

Sl. No.	*Name of the Village*	*Partcipants' Control*		
		Fully Assured	*Fairly Assured*	*Not Assured*
1.	Pulikanmai	39 (97.50)	1 (2.50)	—
2.	Periyakannanur	55 (90.16)	5 (8.19)	1 (1.63)

Source: Computed.

Table 4.19 presents the assurance given by the LCOs on participants' control. To Singhi, the most important reason for the failure of many of the government promoted participatory development programmes is the absence of management control by the participants.[44] People are not accepted as the governors of the programme but they are expected to participate in the programmes governed by outsiders. Ostrom, after studying various participatory institutions concerned with irrigation, has come to the conclusion that the institution must be controlled by the users of the resource.[45] The LCOs in Pulikanmai and Periyakannanur are fully under the control of the village assembly. Most of the respondents in the study area, according to the table, have the confidence that they control the

LCOs. Once the people have this confidence, they do not hesitate to contribute resources to the LCO in the form of money, material and labour and the atmosphere for voluntary contribution without any external coercion emerges.[46] As there is mutual coercion among the participants there is no need for any external coercion. Here there is no scope for any external agency to exploit the contributions made by the participants.

Acting under the Panchayat Act, 1994 and the rules under the Act, Panchayati Raj Institutions have not facilitated people's control over the natural resources. The policy of State control over all natural resources, introduced by the East India Company's Ryotwari land revenue policy, still has its effect. Vani says that the panchayats are expected only to manage the natural resources and not to control the natural resources. At any time any natural resources with the Panchayati Raj Institutions can be taken over by the State. A close study of the rules relating to the irrigation tanks with the panchayats will reveal the fact that the tanks are controlled by the Revenue Department and the Public Works Department. In this context, the Panchayati Raj Institutions are not in a position to give assurance of popular control over resources. Jodha argues that local control gives scope for the use of local community knowledge (LCK) in the management of resources and that LCK plays a very critical role in effectively managing the local resources.[47]

Scholars like Madhav Gadgil have explain how local organisations can save valuable resources for generations with locally evolved institutions.[48] Once local control is removed the people's interest in participation is also reduced.

TABLE 4.20: Assurance by LCOs on Autonomy

Sl. No.	*Name of the Village*	*Autonomous Status*		
		Fully Assured	*Fairly Assured*	*Not Assured*
1.	Pulikanmai	33 (82.50)	6 (15.00)	1 (2.50)
2.	Periyakannanur	51 (83.60)	10 (16.39)	—

Source: Computed.

The assurance given by the LCOs on autonomy is presented in Table 4.20. Most of the respondents from both the study villages, as per the table, say that their LCOs are autonomous in the context of management of natural resources.

Ostrom argues that the local autonomy of the organisation to take operational decisions by the users themselves is very crucial to the success of the organisation. In irrigation management, prudent decisions can be taken only by the users themselves and local community knowledge is essential for decision-making. When the people are permitted to make decisions at the operational level, they have also a commitment to enforce the decisions and to properly monitor the process of enforcement. Institutions which are dominanted by external agencies in the decision-making process have only limited scope for ensuring participation. Such participation can not be sustained over a long period of time. Long enduring institutions are basically self organised systems, wherein the people take the initiative and executive decisions on their own.

Some of the recent studies on the State promoted local bodies have indicated the need for moving from participation to self-governance. Short-term participation can be promoted by the State by offering tempting incentives to the people. Such attempts by the state have been made in Tamil Nadu through a scheme called "Namakku Name" (We for Ourselves). But scholars like Ostrom think in terms of intergenerational participation in conservation of resources. So she talks in terms of long enduring self organised systems.[49]

TABLE 4.21: Assurance by Panchayats on Equity

Sl. No.	*Name of the Village*	*Equity*		
		Fully Assured	*Fairly Assured*	*Not Assured*
1.	Pulikanmai	32 (80.00)	5 (15.00)	2 (5.00)
2.	Periyakannanur	57 (93.44)	4 (6.55)	—

Source: Computed.

In Pulikanmai, the SC farming families also participate in the functioning of the LCO. They are not marginalised. In Pulikanmai, a significant development occurred in the 1996 panchayat election. One general ward in the village was allotted to the SC people by the initiative of the LCO. In return, for the post of President of the village panchayat, the SC people supported a local candidate who was sponsored by the LCO. The LCO tries to accommodate the SC people's interests also.

In Periyakannanur and Pulikanmai, the LCOs do not permit any differences in resources sharing, particularly in sharing water for irrigation. There are no incidents of atrocities against the Scheduled Caste families. During community feasts, the food is shared by all the families. No communal conflicts have been recorded as per the information given by the village administrative officers of both the villages. These are enough indicators to show that caste based exploitation and atrocities are not problems in the study villages.

TABLE 4.22: Assurance by LCOs on Efficiency

Sl. No.	*Name of the Village*	*Efficiency*		
		Fully Assured	*Fairly Assured*	*Not Assured*
1.	Pulikanmai	34 (85.00)	4 (10.00)	2 (5.00)
2.	Periyakannanur	50 (81.96)	10 (16.39)	1 (1.63)

Source: Computed.

The assurance given by the LCOs on efficiency is presented in Table 4.22. Most of the respondents of the study area, according to the table, think that their LCOs are efficient enough to manage the above said functions to the satisfaction of the users.

Organisations should fulfil the requirements of the members to command compliance. Ostrom says, "Although it is impossible to evaluate the efficiency of the systems (self-governing irrigation systems) precisely, the repeated willingless of the users to invest labour and other resources is strong evidence that individual farmers receive more benefits from these systems than the costs they assume for maintaining them."[53]

Ostrom argues that the efficiency of the organisation in serving the interests of the members is the most important evaluative criterion.

For this study efficiency is understood in terms of distribution of water, water scarcity management and conservation of resources and maintenance of boundary. The *kudi* system ensures the relationship between the families' contribution and the benefit the families get. Robert Wade calls such an organisation "Corporate Village Organisation" and such a villages "Corporate Villages".[54] Corporate organisations requires efficiency and must be user friendly.

The LCOs in the study area fulfil the basic requirements of the farming families and accommodate the interests of the non-farming families also. In the Sivagangai area water is a scarce resource. People find it difficult to get even drinking water. Water has to be harvested during the monsoon and must be carefully used.

Here organisational efficiency plays a critical role. It must ensure that every user of the resource contributes to the harvest and in the conservation of the resource it has to check free riders and penalise them by strictly maintaining the boundary. Management of water scarcity is the test of its organisational efficiency. In the absence of efficient sharing of water chances for crop failure are vey high. In such circumstances the organisation must efficiently distribute water to save the crop. Appointment of common irrigators and evolving rules on priority, rotation, duration and frequency of irrigation are some of the steps taken by the LCOs. The evolved rules must be properly enforced. The organisation must command the voluntary compliance of the participants. At times of acute scarcity rules related to water sharing must be introduced to save at least a portion of the standing crop. The LCOs in the study villages are able to meet all these requirements.

Table 4.23 presents the assurance given by the LCOs on stability. The stability of the organisation builds confidence in the minds of the participants and commands better compliance with the rules. Even at the national level, the stability of political institutions plays a key role in commanding popular respect. Only stable institutions can develop and conserve resources like irrigation tanks.

TABLE 4.23: Assurance by Panchayats on Stability

Sl. No.	*Name of the Village*	*Stability*		
		Fully Assured	*Fairly Assured*	*Not Assured*
1.	Pulikanmai	38 (95.00)	2 (5.00)	—
2.	Periyakannanur	57 (93.44)	4 (6.55)	—

Source: Computed.

Historians of the Tamil country have found records showing that such institutions were functioning for hundreds of years efficiently. Inscriptions related to tank and other water bodies in the Tamil country expect institutions to manage them for eternity. In the study area also such temple inscriptions provide evidence of 800-year-old local assemblies managing the resources.[55] Most of the respondents from both the study villages, according to the table, are assured that their LCOs are stable enough to protect the natural resources and the interests of the participants. Discussion with a retired school teacher in Pulikanmai indicated that the LCO in the village has been functioning effectively for many generations. The school building in the village was constructed in 1926 at the initiative of the LCO.

Another reason for the stability of the LCO is the set of conventions, customs and norms practised traditionally. Most of the rules relating to the management of the irrigation tanks have been evolved by years of experimentation. The outcome of such experiments has been converted into customs and norms. The game theorist explains how people learn to cooperate from repeated experiments.[56]

Another advantage of the LCOs in the study area is the process of consensus building in decision-making. The village assembly meetings always work towards consensu and they never take decisions by voting. As there is no process of election, group rivalry is avoided. In Pulikanmai the executive membership is rotated among all the families and the tenure of the membership is one year. Even though the membership is rotated it does not cause destability because the major decision-making powers are with the LCO.

Because of the electoral process, the panchayats are not free from group rivalry and elections breed instability and sustain factionalism.[57]

TABLE 4.24: Assurance by Panchayats on Adaptability

Sl. No.	*Name of the Village*	*Adaptability*		
		Fully Assured	*Fairly Assured*	*Not Assured*
1.	Pulikanmai	36 (90.00)	2 (5.00)	2 (5.00)
2.	Periyakannanur	58 (95.08)	2 (3.27)	1 (1.63)

Source: Computed.

The assurance given by the LCOs on adaptability is presented in Table 4.24. Ostrom and Kenance regard the adaptability of the organisation to the changing requirements as an important evaluative criterion for the institutions managing common natural resources.[58] The management of natural resources is a dynamic process. Changes occur rapidly in the socio-economic and political environment. The condition of natural resources also changes. Because of these changes participants' behaviour also changes. Many traditional institutions are not able to adapt to these changes and they are fast vanishing.

Most of the respondents in both the study villages, as per the table, are confident that the LCOs have the capacity to adapt. The LCOs are dynamic and flexible. Oakerson calls such institutions dynamic institutions of resources management. Both the institutions are not bound by a rigid traditional value system. The people of Pulikanmai decided to remove the authority of the traditional leaders two decades back and introduced a system of rotating the executive committee membership among all the families and the tenure of the membership was reduced to one year. They have also accommodated the SC families within the system. The LCO's activities have been diversified into new areas like establishing a local library in the village, improvement of the performance of the ration shop, noon meal centre and the village school.

In Periyakannanur due to the influence of a leftist political party, a struggle for land reform was launched. In the process of the struggle many of the old values relating to social hierarchy and caste system lost their significance. The SC families of Periyakannanur participate in the village assembly meetings without any restrictions. In the management of the common fund also they have adopted new systems. Bank accounts are kept in the names of three members of the executive committee and it is very difficult to manipulate the money in the bank by an individual.

TABLE 4.25: Assurance by LCOs on Sustainability

Sl. No.	*Name of the Village*	*Sustainability*		
		Fully Assured	*Fairly Assured*	*Not Assured*
1.	Pulikanmai	37 (92.50)	3 (7.50)	—
2.	Periyakannanur	53 (86.88)	7 (11.47)	1 (1.63)

Source: Computed.

Table 4.25 presents the assurance given by the LCOs on sustainability. Oakerson regards the capacity of the institutions to maintain the sustainability of the resources as important in building confidence among the participants.[59] Short-term efficiency or short-term equity is not enough. People in environmentally sensitive areas are much concerned about 'long run efficiency' and intergenerational equity. So Oakerson regards sustainability as a basic evaluating yardstick for institutional efficiency.

Most of the respondents from both the study villages, according to the table, have confidence in their LCOs' ability to use the resource sustainability.

People in Pulikanmai and Periyakannanur are dependent on their irrigation tanks for their economic survival. So they have conserved their tanks for generations and got benefited from them. They are ready to be the custodians of natural resources if they are permitted to do so. They have developed their own institutions, customs, norms and rules for the conservation and use of the resources on which they depend for their survival.

People of Pulikanmai and Periyakannanur have a long-term

vision about their resources and, to operationalise it, they have developed the LCO. Keeping sustainability in mind, the people of both the villages have collectively decided to forego some short-term gains. The conservation of trees in both the villages is the most attractive development noticed by any visitor to the villages. In Pulikanmai village one can see hundreds of tamarind trees. In both the villages common lands have a green cover. The tank bunds of both the villages have a rich growth of trees and plants. Such green cover helps conservation of top soil, controls soil erosion and prevents silting of the water bodies.

To achieve these developments, the LCOs have had to impose some harsh decisions on the people like the ban on goat rearing and the regulation of grazing. Goat rearing is a profitable venture in villages, but very harmful to the ecology of the villages. The achievement of the LCOs shows the institutions' strength and their acceptability to the people. Because of repeated maintenance work in the tanks by the LCOs, proper rain harvesting has been possible in both the villages.

TABLE 4.26: Assurance by LCOs on Transparency and Accountability

Sl. No.	*Name of the Village*	*Transparency and Accountability*		
		Fully Assured	*Fairly Assured*	*Not Assured*
1.	Pulikanmai	38 (95.00)	2 (5.00)	—
2.	Periyakannanur	51 (83.60)	8 (13.11)	2 (3.27)

Source: Computed.

In Periyakannanur village the common funds are managed by the village assembly and handled by the executive committee. A major portion of the common fund is deposited in a Cooperative Bank in a joint account in the name of the members of the executive committee. The first item on the agenda in every village assembly meeting is the submission of accounts.

The success of the LCOs in both the villages largely depends on the transparency and accountability maintained by them.

Participation

The study is an attempt to test the participation of people facilitated by institutions. Participation is not a pipe dream but a reality, as pointed out by scholars like Wade, Ostrom, Jodha, Baland and Platteau. Ostrom argues that the participation of the people depends on the facilitating role of the institutions. By providing assurance, institutions facilitate long enduring participation. The management of natural resources requires participation by successive generations. For this study nine evaluating indicators of participation facilitated by the institutions are identified. These nine indicators are identified from field experience and in the light of Ostrom's design principles for self-governing long enduring institutions for managing irrigation works. Here the respondents have been asked to identify their participation in the management of the irrigation tanks and other related natural resources facilitated by the panchayats and the LCOs. The study indicates that the scope for people's participation depends on institutional arrangement. Approprate institutions are able to facilitate people's participation. The data collected is analysed here against the background of Ostrom's framework for long enduring self-governing institutions.

Participation Facilitated by Panchayats

Table 4.27 presents the participation of the respondents in Gram Sabha meetings. Article 243 A of the Indian Constitution and Section 3 of the Tamil Nadu Panchayat Act, 1994 have created a Gram

TABLE 4.27: Participation in Gram Sabha Meetings

Sl. No.	*Name of the Village*	*Participation in Gram Sabha Meetings*		
		Regularly	*Some times*	*Never*
1.	Pulikanmai	2 (5.00)	3 (7.50)	35 (87.50)
2.	Periyakannanur	4 (6.55)	9 (14.75)	48 (78.68)

Source: Computed.

Sabha in every village panchayat. The approval of village plan is one of the major functions of the Gram Sabha as per the Act of 1994. Development of agriculture, including minor irrigation works, watershed, wasteland, and forestry development are the areas in which village panchayats can plan. There is also provision in the Act to hand over the natural resources under the control of the panchayat union and the Revenue Department to the village panchayat for the benefit of the local community. Such issues can be taken up as part of the village panchayat plan in the Gram Sabha meetings.

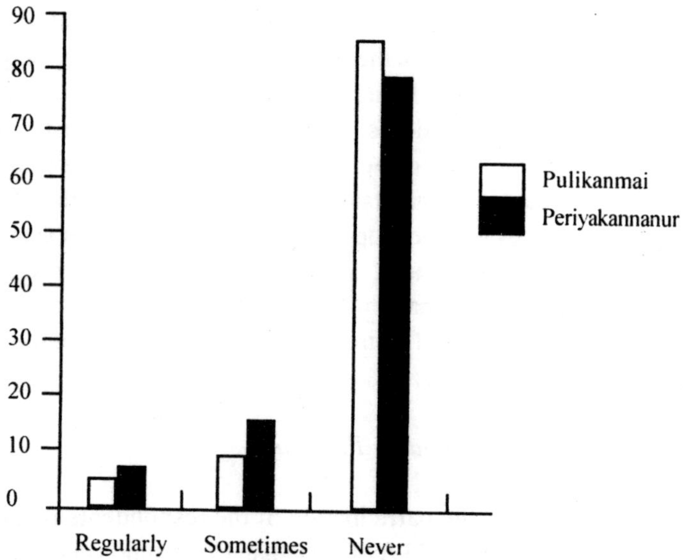

Fig. 4.2 : Participation of Respondents in Gram Sabha Meetings.

But most of the respondents of Pulikanmai and Periyakannanur did not participate in the meetings of the Gram Sabha. A villager told the researcher that he did not attend the Gram Sabha meetings because it did not give him any benefit. Only the panchayat President, the members and the people connected with them attended the meetings of the Gram Sabha. The President of the Periyakannanur told the researcher that Gram Sabha meetings were held to satisfy the government orders. From Pulikanmai, only very few people attended the meetings and the panchayat President admitted that he offered refreshments to the participants as an incentive. The major problem associated with the Gram Sabha meeting is the size and the heterogeneous nature of its members. For example, Periyakannanur has eleven villages and hamlets and people may not have interest enough to travel from distant villages to attend the meeting.

TABLE 4.28 : Participation in Decision-Making Process in Panchayats

Sl. No.	*Name of the Village*	*Village Panchayat*			*Panchayat Union*		
		Well	*Satisfactory*	*No*	*Well*	*Satisfactory*	*No*
1.	Pulikanmai	—	4 (10.00)	36 (90.00)	—	1 (2.50)	39 (97.50)
2.	Periyakannanur	—	5 (8.19)	56 (91.80)	—	2 (3.27)	59 (96.72)

Source: Computed.

The participation of the respondents in the decision-making process in the panchayats is presented in Table 4.28. Section 133(2) of the Tamil Nadu Panchayat Act, 1994 says, "The village panchayat or the panchayat union council shall have power, subject to such restrictions and control as may be prescribed, to executive kudimaramathu in respect of any irrigation source in the village and to levy such fee and on such basis for the purpose thereof as may be prescribed."

Section 133(1) specifies the functions of protection, maintenance, management of turns of irrigation and the regulation of distribution of water to the fields. Under this section the Government has transferred tanks having less than 100 acres of irrigated land to the panchayat union and tanks having less than 10 acres of irrigated land to the village panchayats. A total of 31,678 irrigation tanks have been transferred to the panchayats as per the Act. Most of the respondents from both the study villages, as per the table, said that they have never influenced the panchayat union council or the village panchayat in matters relating to the management of tanks. Discussions with the respondents revealed the fact that most of them were ignorant that the panchayat union or the village panchayat can organise kudimaramathu and manage the distribution of water. The panchayat union councillors never visited the villages after the elections. So there was no opportunity for the people to discuss issues like tank management with them. On verfication with the officials of the panchayat union council, it was found that the above mentioned issues were never taken up for discussion in the last two and a half years by the panchayat union council.

An elderly farmer in the Pulikanmai village told the researcher that they did not want the panchayat union to take up such matters when such things could be better decided at the village level itself.

TABLE 4.29: Participation Facilitated by Panchayats in the Maintenance of Irrigation Tanks

Sl. No.	*Name of the Village*	*Tank Maintenance*		
		Regularly	*Sometimes*	*Never*
1.	Pulikanmai	—	2 (5.00)	38 (95.00)
2.	Periyakannanur	—	4 (6.55)	57 (93.44)

Source: Computed.

Table 4.29 presents the respondents' participation, as facilitated by the panchayats, in the maintenance of irrigation tanks. For effective water harvesting, water bodies have to be kept free from silting, wild growth of plants and bushes and damage to physical structures. There are no statutory irrigation grants from the Government to the village panchayats or the panchayat unions. It is clear that the panchayat union is not expected to meet any expenditure from its own funds. But the panchayat union and the village panchayat can levy kudimaramathu fee as per the Act. But its operationalisation remains to be seen.[61]

No respondent from the two study villages, according to the table, participated in any such work organised by the panchayats. The panchayats did not levy kudimaramathu fee from the farmers. The village panchayats did not take any steps to clean any water bodies under their control for their improvement with people's participation. From discussions with the local people it was found that such work was done by the panchayats normally through contractors.

TABLE 4.30: Participation Facilitated by Panchayats in the Emergency Repair of Irrigation Tanks

Sl. No.	*Name of the Village*	*Emergency Repair Work*		
		Regularly	*Sometimes*	*Never*
1.	Pulikanmai	—	—	40 (100.00)
2.	Periyakannanur	—	—	61 (100.00)

Source: Computed.

The participation of the respondents, as facilitated by the panchayats, in the emergency repair of tanks is presented in Table 4.30. Section 133 of the Act of 1994 expects the village panchayat and the local community to attend to emergency repair of the physical structures of tanks as per the Compulsory Labour Act of 1858 enacted under Company Rule.[62] Even after 150 years, the Act of 1858 has validity. Without being given the power to manage the local irrigation tank, the local community is expected to attend to emergency repair of tanks in times of floods. It is a colonial policy retained by the State even after Independence.[63]

All the respondents, as per the table, said that they never participated in any such emergency repair work undertaken by the village panchayat in the irrigation tank. In both the study villages such emergency repairs have been undertaken in the recent past by the LCO and people have participated in the work. Such emergency operations have to be undertaken immediately. The panchayats, the Revenue Department and the Public Works Department cannot attend to such repairs in emergencies with people's participation. Only the local community can undertake such operations. The Act of 1858 recognised this fact, but the colonial law makers tried to transfer the responsibility of maintenance work to the local community without the right to manage the resource. People will not accept such an irrational proposal from the State.

TABLE 4.31: Participation Facilitated by Panchayats in the Distribution of Water

Sl. No.	*Name of the Village*	*Water Distribution*		
		Regularly	*Sometimes*	*Never*
1.	Pulikanmai	—	—	40 (100.00)
2.	Periyakannanur	—	—	61 (100.00)

Source: Computed.

Table 4.31 presents the respondents' participation, as facilitated by the panchayat, in the distribution of water. By law the panchayat can distribute water from the tank to the field. In both Pulikanmai and Periyakannanur villages no such distribution work by the village panchayat or the panchayat union has ever taken place. All the respondents said that they never participated in any such efforts by the panchayats for distribution of water.

Water distribution is a very sensitive issue in these two villages. People cannot tolerate any mismanagement of water distribution. So they do not want to hand over these types of responsibilities to the panchayats. Ostrom asserts the need for the management of distribution by the beneficiaries themselves.[64] The panchayat union or even the village panchayat cannot undertake any such work. Sengupta also found the inability of formal arrangements to attend to such work.[65] In this context, the LCOs do the work in the study area to the satisfaction of the people. A study by Palanithurai in Tamil Nadu also has found that not only the people but also the elected leaders of the panchayats think that the panchayats give more importance to agency functions than to the management of common property resources.[66]

The participation of the respondents, as facilitated by the panchayats in the management of water scarcity, is presented in Table 4.32. Section 133 of the Panchayat Act, 1994 and the rules under the section give powers to regulate the turns of water and the distribution of water. The panchayats can decide the order of priority, the time of irrigation, the duration of irrigation and the total quantity

TABLE 4.32: Participation Facilitated by Panchayats in Management of Water Scarcity

Sl. No.	*Name of the Village*	*Management of Water Scarcity*		
		Regularly	*Sometimes*	*Never*
1.	Pulikanmai	—	—	40 (100.00)
2.	Periyakannanur	—	—	61 (100.00)

Source: Computed.

of water to be released for irrigation. It can appoint the required staff to attend to such functions. It can control the common irrigators.

Such functions would be very useful for scarcity management of irrigation tanks. But, in practice, no such functions have been undertaken by the panchayats in the study area. All the respondents from both the villages, as per the table, admitted that they have never participated in any such work. The discussions with the respondents indicated that water scarcity is a people's problem affecting their economic survival and so they do not want the panchayats to attend to such critical functions. As Wade points out, direct people's participation at the village level is possible at times of scarcity and risk.[67] In the study villages, proper sharing of water in an equitable and fair manner has been done by the community itself for a long period of time. The panchayats, as part of the government machinery, may find it difficult to take up such responsibility. "Any mismanagement of water sharing at times of scarcity may result in conflicts and violence in rural areas," an elderly farmer told the researcher. Because of these reasons the respondents are not very enthusiastic about participation in the sharing of water through the panchayats.

Table 4.33 presents the respondents' participation, as facilitated by the panchayats, in the conservation of trees. Under Section 134 (1), (2), (3) and (4), the panchayats can develop and conserve trees in the common lands in the village. In irrigation tanks also they can develop forestry for the benefit of the public. Most of respondents, according to the table, stated that they never participated in any such

TABLE 4.33: Participation Facilitated by Panchayats in Conservation of Trees

Sl. No.	*Name of the Village*	*Conservation of Trees*		
		Regularly	*Sometimes*	*Never*
1.	Pulikanmai	—	4 (10.00)	36 (90.00)
2.	Periyakannanur	—	—	61 (100.00)

Source: Computed.

efforts by the panchayats in conserving trees in the common land in their villages. Discussions revealed that the social forestry plantations in the irrigation tanks in both the study villages were harvested a few years back without any benefit to the local community. The panchayat union did not attempt to involve the local people in the management of the social forestry plantations. During that period the people were not permitted to collect fuel or fodder from the tank by the social forestry officials.

In many panchayats money from the social forestry scheme mostly benefited the Forest Department and the panchayat union. The money given to the village panchayats was used for the general expenditure of the panchayats.[68]

Many village panchayat Presidents have expressed their dissatisfaction with the government policy towards the revenue generated from forest resources in the irrigation tank.[69]

The panchayats practically do not have any integrated approach to the ecological development of the villages. So they do not bother to develop green cover in the villages. The panchayats' approach is dominated by the policy of revenue generation through forestry.[70]

Scholars like Chambers think that, in State promoted forest schemes in rural areas, local people are not benefited. Indeed the poor often have been losers because they are not permitted to enjoy the rights to collect fuel and fodder from forests developed by the panchayats. The concentration of such programmes are mostly on urban needs like pulp, poles and commercial fuel.[71]

Because of these reasons local people are not interested in participating in any of the government programmes like social forestry. Instead the people in the study area use their LCO to conserve the trees in the village common land.

TABLE 4.34: Participation Facilitated by Panchayats in the Regulation of Grazing

Sl. No.	*Name of the Village*	*Regulation of Grazing*		
		Regularly	*Sometimes*	*Never*
1.	Pulikanmai	—	—	40 (100.00)
2.	Periyakannanur	—	—	61 (100.00)

Source: Computed.

The participation of the respondents, as facilitated by the panchayats, in the regulation of grazing is presented in Table 4.34. Under Section 134 (2), (4) and (5) of the Act of 1994, the village panchayat can regulate grazing in the common lands. Under Section 120 of the Act, grazing in the unreserved forests also can be regulated by the panchayat.

Regulation of grazing is regarded as very important for conserving the land and water resources. Due to heavy cattle grazing many water bodies have been fully destroyed by siltation.[72] Farmers of Sivagangai district are well aware of the fact.

In both the study villages, the respondents, as per the table, have never participated in any of the measures taken by the village panchayats to regulate grazing in the village common land. The panchayat Presidents of both the village expressed their inability to take such steps as per the provisions of the Act. Jodha argues, "Panchayats' dependence on community votes, compelling them to avoid unpopular steps like enforcing CPR user obligations... make the new institutions ineffective."[73] As cattle rearing is an income generating activity and government schemes promote such activities under self-employment programmes, the panchayats cannot enforce strict regulations on grazing in local areas. But the LCOs, with the support of the village assembly, are able to take such decisions and enforce them effectively.

TABLE 4.35: Participation Facilitated by Panchayats in the Conservation and Use of Fisheries in the Irrigation Tanks

Sl. No.	*Name of the Village*	*Conservation and Sharing of Fisheries*		
		Regularly	*Sometimes*	*Never*
1.	Pulikanmai	—	—	40 (100.00)
2.	Periyakannanur	—	—	61 (100.00)

Source: Computed.

Table 4.35 presents the respondents' participation as facilitated by the panchayats, in the conservation and the use of fisheries in the irrigation tanks. Section 133 (3) of the Panchayat Act of 1994 and the rules under the Act regulate the use of fisheries by the panchayats. The rules say that the revenue generated from the fisheries can be spent on improvement of the irrigation tank, agricultural development and the development of fisheries. A careful reading of the Act reveals that the Act and the rules visualise fisheries as a source of revenue for the concerned panchayat. The rights have to be sold in public auction to the highest bidder. Such decisions are taken and implemented by the District Collector and the Revenue Department. The revenue generated from the resources goes to the respective departments or panchayats. No respondent from the study are, according to the table, participated in any efforts by the panchayats to develop fisheries in the irrigation tanks or any other water bodies. The village panchayats have not taken any effort to develop fisheries in their water bodies with the help of the local people. The 73rd Constitutional Amendment Act and Article 243 G of the Constitution expect the panchayats to take steps for planning for economic development including the development of fisheries in villages. But the Tamil Nadu Panchayat Act of 1994 still follows the British land revenue policy introduced under the Permanent Land Revenue Settlement. As Vani argues, panchayat management of resources is still at the conceptual level.[74] Because of the Government's policy, the local people are denied a valuable food resource available in their own village.[75] Traditionally local people harvest the fish in the water bodies in their village for personal consumption. In many villages of Sivaganga district people get fish for personal consumption for a few weeks in a year from the tanks. If it is auctioned the fishes are taken to the markets of nearby cities and towns. In this context people have a temptation to free ride or steal the fish in the water bodies.

TABLE 4.36: Participation in Village Assembly Meetings

Sl. No.	*Name of the Village*	*Participation in Village Asembly Meetings*		
		Regularly	*Some times*	*Never*
1.	Pulikanmai	36 (90.00)	4 (10.00)	—
2.	Periyakannanur	61 (100.00)	—	—

Source: Computed.

Participation Facilitated by LCOs

The respondents' participation in the village assembly meetings, as facilitated by the LCOs, is presented in Table 4.36. Both in Pulikanmai and Periyakannanur, participation in the village assembly is compulsory for the members. Failure to attend attracts penaly. So most of the respondents in both the villages of the study area, as per the table, are regular in attending meetings. Issues like the management of irrigation tanks and other common natural resources, minor disputes, village development activities and village festivals are normally discussed in the village assembly meetings. Because of the absence of a landed aristocracy in the study villages, dominance by any individual in the meetings is not possible. However, the gender dominance in the meeting is obvious. In Periyakannanur village all the Scheduled Caste families have lands and so they are able to participate like any other caste group. In Pulikanmai village, only twelve SC families have land in the tank area and only these 12 SC families participate in the village assembly meetings. The landless SC families do not take part in meetings specifically arranged to discuss issues related to the management of irrigation tanks. In Pulikanmai there are five landless BC families and they also do not take part in discussions related to tank management. But all the families participate in discussions on matters related to regulation of grazing, community fishing, ban on goat rearing and protection of trees.

As the LCO is a need based organisation, people are interested only in issues directly affecting them. As all the villagers have to abide by the rules framed by the village assembly, all the families consider attendance at the meeting very important. As issues like sharing of water from the irrigation tank which affect the economic survival of the families are discussed in the village assembly meeting, every one is very keen on attending the village assembly meetings and taking part in the discussions.

TABLE 4.37: Participation in Decision-Making Process

Sl. No.	*Name of the Village*	*Participation in Decision-Making Process*		
		Regularly	*Sometimes*	*Never*
1.	Pulikanmai	36 (90.00)	3 (7.50)	1 (12.50)
2.	Periyakannanur	58 (95.08)	3 (4.91)	—

Source: Computed.

Table 4.37 presents the respondents' participation in the decision-making process as facilitated by the LCOs. Most of the respondents from both the study villages participate in the decision-making process in the LCOs on issues related to the management of natural resources. The village assembly is practically a social group of users with clear boundaries. The membership is restricted to the people affected by the decisions. So the participants are interested in involving themselves in the decision-making process. In both the villages it is found that the decision-making body is the village assembly. No decision can be taken without the knowledge of the village assembly. Decisions require the cooperation and contribution of the members of the LCOs and the LCOs do not have any other outside support to rely upon. In this context, the members alone have control over the decision-making process. The executive committee has the responsibility to execute the decisions. On urgent problems, the executive committee may be required to take spot decisions. But such decisions need ratification by all the members. Such an arrangement gives a good deal of scope for people to participate directly and indirectly in the decision-making process.

TABLE 4.38: Participation Facilitated by LCOs in Maintenance of Irrigation Tanks

Sl. No.	*Name of the Village*	*Participation in Maintenance Work*		
		Regularly	*Sometimes*	*Never*
1.	Pulikanmai	32 (80.00)	2 (5.00)	6 (15.00)
2.	Periyakannanur	61 (100.00)	—	—

Source: Computed.

Table 4.38 presents the respondents' participation, as facilitated by the LCOs, in the maintenance of the irrigation tanks. In Periyakannanur village, as all families have land in the irrigated area, all the families participate in the annual maintenance work. In Pulikanmai village families which do not have land in the tank area are not required to participate. But sometimes a few landless families also participate in the annual maintenance work as it is considered a community event. Youth and children of the village also join the formal team of workers in the maintenance work. However, those who have land in the irrigated area have to participate compulsory in the annual clearance of the supply channel. If the annual clearance is not properly done, the flow of water to the tank will be affected. If the tank does not get enough water, the paddy cultivation will be affected. Good paddy harvest will benefit even the landless in the village also. During the harvest season even landless families of Pulikanmai village can get around four hundred kilograms of paddy as wages. Small farmers and marginal farmers help one another in harvesting and get paddy as wages. A good crop in the village gives food security to a great extent to each and every family. So the landless families also show interest in the proper maintenance of the tank. Not only in Pulikanmai and Periyakannanur but in many villages of Tamil Nadu, particularly in Sivagangai and Ramnad districts, community maintenance of irrigation tanks is a normal practice and cases are recorded by Palanisamy[76] and Nirmal Sengupta.[77] As Sengupta points out, "participation of farmers in the tank management was a very evident reality in the field but totally neglected area of reportage". Sengupta adds, "annual repairs are therefore still unertaken by beneficiaries themselves on their own".[78] It proves that collective action for common good is still a reality in some pockets of rural areas in India wherever conditions are favourable and where formal or informal organisations are operating.

TABLE 4.39: Participation Facilitated by LCOs in Emergency Repair of Irrigation Tanks

Sl. No.	*Name of the Village*	*Participation in Emergency Repair Work*		
		Regularly	*Sometimes*	*Never*
1.	Pulikanmai	36 (90.00)	4 (10.00)	—
2.	Periyakannanur	61 (100.00)	—	—

Source: Computed.

The participation of the respondents, as facilitated by the LCOs, in the emergency repair of irrigation tanks is presented in Table 4.39. Section 133 of the Tamil Nadu Panchayat Act expects the village panchayat and the village community to attend to emergency work in tanks during floods. Breaches of tank structures during floods are frequent in irrigation tanks. Particularly in Sivagangai District, with its sandy soil, tank bunds are prone to breaches. The Public Works Department, the Revenue Department and the panchayat union cannot get information in time on breach of tanks and react rapidly. Constant watch over tank bunds during floods can be maintained only by the local community. It is because of this that the Compulsory Labour Act, 1858, which gives the local community the duty of attending to emergency repair work in tanks, is kept alive even today in the Panchayat Act of 1994. This section and a few other sections of the Act half-heartedly accept the role of the community in managing natural resources.

In both villages, as per the table, all the respondents attend to emergency repair work in the tanks during floods. In both the villages, during recent years, such breaches of the tank bunds occurred during floods. In such situations, the entire village community, including women and children, joined in the repair operations. Breach of tank during floods affects not only the landowners but the entire village community. It is a threat to the entire village, houses, cattle and other properties of the village. The LCOs are able to use the spontaneous participation of the people in such situations effectively to repair the tank structures.

TABLE 4.40: Participation Facilitated by LCOs in Distribution of Water

Sl. No.	*Name of the Village*	*Participation in Water Distribution*		
		Regularly	*Sometimes*	*Never*
1.	Pulikanmai	32 (80.00)	2 (5.00)	6 (15.00)
2.	Periyakannanur	61 (100.00)	—	—

Source: Computed.

Table 4.40 presents the respondents' participation, as facilitated by the LCOs, in the distribution of water. Efficient distribution of water to the fields of the farmers is the key to the success of the organisation. Ostrom points out, "The repeated willingness of the users to invest labour and other resources is strong evidence that individual farmers receive more benefits from these systems than the cost they assume for maintaining them".[79] According to Ostrom, the distribution of water must be done efficiently and distribution by farmers themselves will ensure this.[80] Most of the respondents in both the study villages, according to the table, stated that they participate in the distribution of water. As per the Act the distribution of water may be done by the panchayats. But, in practice, nowhere in Tamil Nadu does any panchayat union or village panchayat do so.

In the study villages, the rules governing the distribution of water are collectively decided by people in the village assembly. To operationalise the rules framed, common irrigators are appointed by the village assembly. The functioning of the common irrigators is discussed in the village assembly. In Pulikanmai the common irrigators are paid by the LCO. In both the villages, the wages for the common irrigators are fixed by the village assembly. Any misuse of water can be reported to the village assembly by any member for discussion. During the irrigation season the village assembly meetings are conducted frequently in both the villages and the distribution of water is collectively monitored. Ostrom asserts the need for close monitoring of the distribution of resources by the users themselves to minimize opportunities available to individuals to free ride, shirk or break the rules without detection.[81]

No external agency can do local distribution of water to the satisfaction of the users. The appointment of common irrigators by the village assembly for distribution of water is vital for managing water scarcity. The distribution done by the common irrigators is expected to be objective. In some villages of Ramnad and Sivagangai districts, a practice is followed to ensure the impartiality of the common irrigators. In one village, after their appointment, the common irrigators are taken to the temple for taking an oath to remain impartial. With this oath they break a coconut.[82] Community based institutions have several systems of checks and balances to ensure that the water is distributed impartially among all the farmers. Such arrangements require cooperation and consensus among the people. No outside agency promoted by the State or the panchayat union can bring about such an atmosphere. Here tradition, culture, moral norms and sacred sentiments play a key role in bringing about a spirit of cooperation among the people. Only community based organisations can bring about such cooperation and sustain it for a long period.

The respondents' participation, as facilitated by the LCOs, in the management of water scarcity, is presented in Table 4.41. Hardin's theory explains the problem of unregulated competition in resource sharing and the tragic consequence of the decline of valuable natural resources. When resources are scarce, use must be based on rational calculation. Individual competitive exploitation may bring disaster to

TABLE 4.41: Participation Facilitated by LCOs in the Management of Water Scarcity

Sl. No.	Name of the Village	Participation in Water Scarcity Management		
		Regularly	*Sometimes*	*Never*
1.	Pulikanmai	32 (80.00)	—	8 (20.00)
2.	Periyakannanur	61 (100.00)	—	—

Source: Computed.

all because of the total decline of valuable resources. In such situations individual rationality may bring about collective irrationality. Baland and Platteau think that, by experience, individuals learn to cooperate and to avoid such tragic conse-quences.[83] For that they need institutional arrangements to ensure rational distribution of resources to all the stake holders in a fair manner.

In many villages of Tamil Nadu conflicts and violence over the distribution of water for irrigation in times of scarcity are reported. But, in Periyakannanur and Pulikanmai, water scarcity is effectively managed by a system devised by the LCOs.

Most of the respondents, as per the table, said that they partcipate in the management of scarcity of water. It means that they take part in devising schemes for water sharing and make collective arrangements for implementation of the sharing principles and monitoring the process of implementation. The appointment of common irrigators is the first step in the direction of objective water sharing. When water is scarce, the village assembly decides how much land each family can irrigate. In the study villages, in times of acute water scarcity, each family is permitted to irrigate a specific area of land, irrespective of the size of the landholding of the family.

The village assembly decides the maximum land area to be irrigated by a family. A family may have 3 acres of land but the LCO may permit it to irrigate only 0.75 acres. A family may have only 0.5 acre, but it can cultivate its entire landholding. If some family does not want to use its share, they can sell their share of water to any farmer in the tank area and get paddy in return. The system has the following objectives :

1. At least a portion of the standing crop has to be saved by restricting irrigation to a portion of the landholding.
2. Every family in the village must get at least a minimum of its food requirement even in times of acute water scarcity.

This system gives food security to the entire village community to some extent. If a family gets proper harvest from 0.5 acres of land, it can get around 1000 kgs. of paddy, sufficient to save the family from starvation. Such collective wisdom in the villages of Sivagangai district saves many families from starvation.

TABLE 4.42: Participation Facilitated by LCOs in Conservation of Trees

Sl. No.	*Name of the Village*	*Participation in Conservation of Trees*		
		Regularly	*Sometimes*	*Never*
1.	Pulikanmai	38 (95.00)	2 (5.00)	—
2.	Periyakannanur	59 (96.72)	2 (3.27)	—

Source: Computed.

Table 4.42 presents the respondents' participation, as facilitated by the LCOs, in the conservation of trees. Most of the respondents in both the study villages, according to the table, said that they participate in the efforts of the LCO in conserving trees by following the rules evolved by the village assembly. They also monitor the proper implementation of the rules. No one is permitted to cut any trees in the common land. In both the villages, guards have been appointed and are paid from the community fund. The villagers have to collectively monitor the conservation of trees. The villagers are permitted to collect fuel from the thorny bushes from the common lands for their use. Collection of firewood as a source of income is not permitted. Fodder also can be collected from the common lands but not from the trees. Because of these regulations there is a thick growth of green cover and the top soil is protected in both the villages. In Pulikanmai village, every household has trees like neem and tamarind. People have trees in their farm land also. Tamarind trees give good income. A householder from Pulikanmai told the researcher that he gets around Rs. 4,500 from six tamarind trees in his land. The neem and palmyra trees are used as timber. In Pulikanmai village collection of palmyra sap is prohibited because it may be used to produce the intoxicating toddy. Neem nuts are used to get neem oil and neem cake. In both the villages, due to soil condition and scarcity of water, only there is limited scope for agriculture. So the community shows interest in growing trees in common and private lands. The regulations on conservation of trees serve both private and community interests. Without such regulations even trees in private lands cannot be conserved. Here private interest and common interest are perfectly interdependent and the scope for community conservation is very high.

TABLE 4.43: Participation Facilitated by LCOs in Regulation of Grazing

Sl. No.	*Name of the Village*	*Participation in Grazing Regulation*		
		Regularly	*Sometimes*	*Never*
1.	Pulikanmai	40 (100.00)	—	—
2.	Periyakannanur	61 (100.00)	—	—

Source: Computed.

The respondents' participation, as facilitated by the LCOs, in the regulation of grazing is presented in Table 4.43. Grazing regulations significantly affect the condition of the watershed management. Over-grazing is injurious to the health of the watershed. Grazing induces soil erosion, decline of green cover and siltation of water bodies. The Sukhomajri model of watershed management gives evidence for the relationship between unregulated grazing and the health of the water bodies.[84] The regulation of grazing was the first step towards bringing about economic prosperity to the village community in Sukhomajri.

Most of the respondents, as per the table, participate in regulating grazing in their village by evolving rules relating to grazing, following the rules evolved, and, monitoring proper implementation of the rules. Pulikanmai and Periyakannanur are in an ecologically sensitive area. The destruction of the green cover will destroy the health of their water bodies. Even though the villagers are not aware of the scientific reasons associated with regulation of grazing, they know the relationship between grazing and the health of water bodies.

In addition, trees play a significant role in their economy. Particularly, in Pulikanmai village, families get substantial income from tamarind trees. There are two types of rules followed to regulate grazing. In both the villages goat rearing is prohibited. In Pulikanmai, free grazing in the common lands by any animal is prohibited. Only the village assembly can issue permits to individuals to graze animals in the common land. Only during certain months of the year permits to graze animals in the common lands are issued on payment of the prescribed fees. By this policy the LCO is able to control the types of animals, the number of animals, the area of grazing and the duration of grazing in a year. Issuing permits reduces the grazing, saves the green cover and top soil, and, at the same time, generates income for the community fund. In Periyakannanur only goats are prohibited and grazing by other animals is not prohibited. As goats are regarded as a great threat to the environment and agriculture, in many villages of Sivagangai district, goat rearing is strictly prohibited. In other parts of Tamil Nadu, particularly in the forest areas under the control of the Forest Department, over-grazing by goats has become a great threat to forest land and the Forest Department is helpless.[85]

TABLE 4.44: Participation Facilitated by LCOs in Conservation and Use of Fisheries in Irrigation Tanks

Sl. No.	*Name of the Village*	*Participation in Sharing of Fisheries*		
		Regularly	*Sometimes*	*Never*
1.	Pulikanmai	36 (90.00)	4 (10.00)	—
2.	Periyakannanur	61 (100.00)	—	—

Source: Computed.

Table 4.44 presents the respondents' participation, as facilitated by the LCOs, in the conservation and use of fisheries in the irrigation tanks. In Sivagangai district, a large number of irrigation tanks, ponds and other water bodies are located in villages. In some villages these water bodies are used as fish ponds too. After the harvest of crops, normally, on a fixed day, the villagers collectively harvest the fish in the water bodies. This tradition is called 'Vellai Veechu' (hoisting of white flag). It means the tank is open for community fishing.[86] Before Vellai Veechu no one can enter the water for fishing. Unregulated fishing may lead to premature fishing because of greed and competition. As fishing is prohibited for three to four months after the monsoon, proper growth of the fishes in the tank is ensured. In both the study villages common irrigators and guards play a key role in protecting the fish in the tank. In addition, the entire village community is involved in the process of protection of the fisheries. After the harvest is over, on a fixed day, and at a fixed hour, the tank is opened for community fishing.

All the respondents from both the villagers, according to the table, say that they protect and harvest the fisheries in the irrigation tanks. Because they are regarded as a community resource and the benefit goes to the entire community, the involvement of the people comes spontaneously. In Periyakannanur village the fishes are collectively harvested and the entire harvest is equally divided among the *kudis*. In Pulikanmai village individual families harvest fish from the tank directly. In both the villages, for nearly two weeks in a year, the entire village community gets fish for consumption free of cost. The Panchayat Act regards the fisheries in the village water bodies as a source of income for the panchayats. But the people in the study area are able to directly get a very good source of protein rich food for nearly two weeks in a year free of cost. The people in areas like Pulikanmai and Periyakannanur are not economically capable of purchasing fish from the market.

Discussion on Hypotheses

The first hypothesis of the study assumes that, in people's perception, local community organisations give better assurance to people than the panchayats on the management of irrigation tanks.

The second hypothesis of the study assumes that, in people's perception, LCOs facilitate greater participation of the people in the management of irrigation tanks.

The setting for the study are two villages in an ecologically sensitive and economically backward area. In these villages irrigation tanks are crucial for the survival of the people. There is an absence of large disparities in the landholding. Most of the people are small farmers depending on irrigation tanks. These are the two important factors affecting their participation. The absence of caste based factionalism is a social factor to be noted. The entire district has a tradition of community management of irrigation tanks and other natural resources. The hypotheses are discussed here to test their validity in the light of the data collected and presented in chapters three and four. The hypotheses are discussed not only based on the data collected through the structured schedule but also based on the data collected by a variety of other methods suggested by scholars like Jodha.[86]

The purpose is to use the data provided by the people in the form of oral histories, their experiences with different models of collective action, their insights, their vision and their local knowledge of natural resources. Structured schedules and quantitative analysis of data collected through the schedules are not sufficient to understand the research problem and to test the hypotheses. Scholars like Jodha and Chamber are very particular about the use of unconventional methods in understanding such research problems.[87] Against this background the hypotheses are tested with the available data and deductions are made.

Assurance

As Wade and Ostrom have pointed out, assurance plays the most important role in determining the people's voluntary participation for collective good. Against this background the study has made an attempt to test the hypotheses evolved for the study on assurance. For this purpose 10 indicators of assurance have been evolved. A comparison of the ability of the institutions to provide assurance to the respondents is attempted here.

Protection of Interests

Most of the respondents say that they think that the LCOs protect their interests relating to irrigation tanks and other natural resources. Most of the respondents do not think that their interests are properly protected by the panchayats. Ostrom has pointed out that, in many similar cases, organisations of users of a resource provide better assurance to the users on protection of their interests.[88] The panchayats do not focus on natural resources management. Jodha says that the panchayats' goals are too diversified and natural resources management is only a very small component of their functions.[89] Jodha thinks that the panchayats are political bodies with very little concern for or involvement in natural resources management and that they are interested only in getting money from the Government in the name of natural resources management.[90] Even State policies, dominated by British legacy, regard natural resources as a source of revenue and do not regard them as the base for the survival of the people in the rural areas. As their is not much compatibility of interests between the respondents and the panchayats, the respondents do not think that panchayats can protect their interests.

Assurance of Maintenance of Boundary

Most of the respondents do not think that the panchayats are able to maintain boundary in the management of natural resources. Most of them are fully confident that the LCOs are able to maintain boundary in natural resources management. Maintenance of boundary means the restriction of the use of a resource to the genuine members. The panchayats are not able to enforce such control. They cannot impose conditions, levy contributions and exclude free riders. In fact, the panchayats encourage free riders. Jodha argues that the panchayats convert valuable common natural resources into open access resources and bring about the tragedy of commons.[91] In the name of the panchayat, powerful and rich people can extract resources from the villages. Some valuable resources like sand in the channels, streams and river beds in many villages of Tamil Nadu are exploited thus. The State and the panchayats are not able to restrict such exploitation and, in many villages, this has brought about ecological disaster.[92] But, in places where community organisations are strong, restrictions are imposed. Ostrom considers maintenance of boundary as a very important duty of an institution.[93] She argues that not only avoiding non-members but also enforcing the regulation on members is a very important component of maintenance of boundary. In this study it is found that, in people's perception, the panchayats are not able to maintain boundary property but the LCOs are able to maintain boundary.

Assurance on Control over Organisation

To Ostrom the question of who controls the institution determines people's interest in participation. People need the assurance that they can control the institution which demands participation from them. Most of the respondents of the study villages believe that they control the LCOs in their villages. But they do not think that they can control the Panchayati Raj Institutions. In the context of natural resources management, they are not able to influence the decision-making process in the panchayats. Practically the people of Pulikanmai and Periyakannanur do not keep in touch with their panchayat union councillors after the elections. Even the village panchayat Presidents admit that they do not have any control over the process of natural resource management by the panchayat union. People do not know what the panchayats are doing. The village panchayat does not know what the panchayat union is doing. The panchayat union councillors do not know what the village panchayats are doing. It is a strange arrangement in the Tamil Nadu Panchayat Act, 1994. In total, people practically do not have any control over these institutions in general and more particularly in the area of management of irrigation tanks and other natural resources. A careful study of the Act shows that the real power to control the process of decision-making in the panchayats lies with the State. Particularly, the District Collector has enormous powers to control the process of decision-making on issues relating to natural resources management.

Assurance on Autonomous Status of Organisation

Most of the respondents from both the villages do not think that the panchayats are autonomous enough to manage the natural resources with people's participation. But most of the respondents think that the LCOs are autonomous institutions and that they can manage the natural resources without any outside control.

For long enduring participation, Ostrom asserts that people need self-governing institutions. The Panchayat Act, 1994 says that the panchayats are self-governing participatory institutions. But most of the respondents from the study villages do not think so. On the contrary, they think that the LCOs are autonomous. Ostrom argues that, if an organisation is externally controlled, participation cannot be sustained. Jodha calls the panchayats proxy institutions of the state.[94] The Government uses the panchayats to justify its control over natural resources in which local people have a stake.[95] As far as resource management is concerned, Vani argues that the panchayats have to work within the framework given by the British colonial policies.[96]

A close study of the Tamil Nadu Panchayat Act of 1994 and the rules on management of natural resources indicates that control over natural resource management lies ultimately with the government officials. People's representatives are involved in the process but the decision makers are the government officials. In people's perception, the panchayats are not their institutions with autonomy for self-governance. Even though the Tamil Nadu Panchayat Act, 1994 says, in its introduction, that 'panchayats are self-governing and participatory,' in reality, they are not so. As Vani has pointed out, sections relating to natural resource management in the Panchayat Act are much influenced by the colonial policies.[97]

Assurance on Efficiency of Management

Efficiency in the management of water and other natural resources affects the survival of the people in Pulikanmai and Periyakannanur. It includes maintenance of tank structure, harvest of rain water, distribution of water, scarcity management of water, conservation of trees, and regulation of grazing.

Most of the respondents from the villages regard the LCOs as more efficient in the management of natural resources than the panchayats. Ostrom says that the repeated participation of people in the efforts of local self-governing institutions for several decades is a strong evidence of the capacity of the institutions to provide aussrance to the people on their ability to manage the resources efficiently.[98] In an environmentally sensitive area like the study area, people need assurance on the institution's efficiency in managing fragile resources. Only such an assurance can ensure the participation of the people on a sustainable basis. Participants see whether the institutions are able to maintain proportional equivalence between the benefits and the costs. If the institutions are not able to maintain it, people's interest in participation will decline.

Assurance on Stability of the Organisation

Most of the respondents from both the study villages think that the LCOs give better assurance on the stability of institutional arrangements for management of common property resources than the Panchayati Raj Institutions. Ostrom says that a long enduring system is one that has been in operation for at least several generations.[99] Pulikanmai has had a stable LCO for several decades. In Periyakannanur the LCO has been functioning smoothly for more than thirty-five years.

Panchayats in India are not permitted to function with stability because of frequent changes in government policies. Particularly, the policies of the government relating to natural management are not clear and are often changed to meet the requirements of the State. Political rivalry, factionalism and the involvement of politicians and contractors do not permit the panchayats to have a stable approach to natural resource management. In this context the people of both the villages think that the LCOs are more stable than the panchayats.

Assurance on Equity

To most of the respondents of Pulikanmai and Periyakannanur villages, the LCO gives better assurance on equity. Most of the respondents do not think that the panchayats give them assurance on equity. The *kudi* system in both the villages ensures that, when resources are scarce, they will be distributed equally among the responents. The rules of managing water scarcity practised by the LCOs not only ensure equity but favour families with very little area of land. The Arabari experiments in West Bengal and the Sukhomajri model show the importance of the capacity of the institutions to give assurance on equity in facilitating people's participation.[100] The land reform movement in Periyakannanur played an important role in bringing the SC families into the LCO. Because of the fairness in the functioning of the LCOs in the study area, people's participation is sustained.

On the contrary, the benefits from the panchayats can be got by only the people who are politically well connected and economically strong.[101] In this context it can be said that, in people's perception, the LCOs in the study area give better assurance than the panchayats on equity in distribution.

Assurance on Sustainability

Scholars like Ostrom,[102] Gadgil and Guha[103] have studied the relationship between people's participation and the capacity of institutions to sustain natural resources. In the perception of most of the respondents, the LCOs give better assurance on sustainability of the natural resources than the panchayats. The prople of the study area use the resources prudently through their LCOs with a futuristic vision. The regulation of the use of water, regulations on the use of trees, regulations on grazing and ban on goat rearing are designed by the LCOs with the objective of ensuring sustainability. A few of the regulations like the ban on goat rearing may affect the interests of individuals, because goat rearing is a profitable economic activity. But unregulated goat rearing may destroy the green cover and the ecology of the watershed area. The LCOs of the study area are able to enforce the ban on goat rearing in a way acceptable to the people. The panchayats have short-term vision. The panchayats approach forestry as an income generation venture. They do not appreciate the ecological implications of forestry and, in this context, the social forestry scheme is a very good example.

Assurance of Adaptability

Natural resources management is a dynamic process. The social situation in the villages is also fast changing. Particularly, in districts like Sivagangai, agriculture is a very risky venture because of sporadic rainfall and absence of assured water supply and water scarcity. Here institutional ability to manage unpredictable situations is very significant.[104] The majority of the respondents from both the villages think that the LCOs are more adaptable to changing situations than the Panchayati Raj Institutions. In unpredictable situations, flexibility of rules and regulations is required to meet the situation and save the people from the crisis. Ostrom considers adoptability a very important evaluate criterion for institutional evaluation.[105] Institutions which do not meet the changing needs cannot fulfil the requirements of the people. The panchayats are governed by rules framed elsewhere. Their local adaptability, particularly in the area of natural resource management, is very limited. But the LCOs of the study area are highly flexible. The LCOs play a very important role in changing the attitude of the local peopple towards the SC people. In Periyakannanur village all the SC people have been integrated into the village community. Such adaptability of the LCOs contributes to the sustained participation of the local people.

Assurance on Transparancy and Accountability

Most of the respondents from both the study villages think that the LCOs give better assurance on transparency and accountability in the management of natural resources than the panchayats. Ostrom argues that accountability is one of the most important assurances the participants require from an institution.[105] The panchayats have not activated the Gram Sabha, and, accountability to people and transparency are still a distant vision. The accountability of the panchayats to government agencies, instead of making the panchayats accountable has made them more corrupt. The proposed 'Right to Information' Act in India has yet to come even though various development groups demand it.[106] But, in Pulikanmai and Periyakannanur, the use of resources and common funds is fully transparent. As the decisions are taken in open meetings of the village assembly and accounts are periodically submitted to the village assembly, possibilities for misuse of resources and funds are very limited. Social auditing of not only community funds but also of use of resources has been facilitated consistently by the LCOs of Pulikanmai and Periyakannanur.

The testing of the hypotheses of the study with the available data shows that, in the perception of the people, the LCOs provide better assurance to people than the panchayats in the management of the panchayat irrigation tanks.

Participation

Collective action pessimists think that the scope for participatory management of natural resources is very limited. But some scholars have found that participation is not a pipe dream but a reality in certain specific contexts. Ostrom gives importance to the role of institutional arrangements in facilitating participation. To her, by designing institutions properly, participation can be induced. Wade gives importance to institutional sensitivity to the problems of risk and scarcity which affect people's participation. For this study participation in the panchayats and the LCOs is tested with the help of a set of indicators. The data collected on participation are discussed hereunder against the hypotheses.

Participation in Meetings

The study shows that the participation of the respondents in Gram

Sabha meetings is very low but, in the village assembly meetings, participation is almost full. The village assembly meetings are held on local initiative, to discuss certain critical issues affecting their personal economic interests and the collective interests of their village. The participants are restricted to individuals who are affected by the decisions of the village assembly and who contribute to the LCO and follow the regulations prescribed by the organisation. The village assembly of the LCO is a small cohesive group with a specific purpose. The cohesiveness of the group and the commonality of purpose ensure harmonious behaviour among the members participating in the village assembly meetings. A close look at both the villages reveals that the village assemblies are like corporate bodies of responsible shareholders. Ostrom sees the need for opening the boundaries of an organisation only to contributing members. Non-contributors who do not have a stake in a particular issue may not mind destabilising the process of decision-making. In the Gram Sabha all eligible voters of the village panchayat area from many hamlets participate and a boundary cannot be enforced. In view of this the respodents are not interested in taking issues of concern to their village relating to the management of irrigation tanks and natural resources to the Gram Sabha meeting, which operates above their village level. There is need for hamlet level sabhas which can deal with issues affecting a specific group of people living in a village or hamlet.[107] Pant says, "There are communities living in hamlets which have an identity of interest in many matters, particularly in matters of common property resources and natural resources." He argues that such communities residing in hamlets could be empowered by organising them into self-help thrift groups as self-managing and self-regulating bodies. The village assembly is pragmatic, need based and concentrates on issues of specific interest to a community of people who have common interests in the resources on which they depend for their economic survival.

Participation in Decision-Making Process

Most of the respondents from the villages do not think that they influence the decision-making process of the Gram Sabha, the village panchayat or the panchayat union council on matters relating to irrigation tanks and other natural resources. The panchayats are mostly dominated by non-stake holders in the decision-making process. As Palanithurai has found in his study, the panchayats are not able to plan and implement any programmes relating to the management of common properties because of the dominating role of government departments in the decision-making process.[108] Ostrom says that the decision-making process must be under the control of the participants.[109] In matters related to local fragile natural resources, the interested individuals have to take decisions, implement the decisions and monitor their proper implementation. If they can have an organisation locally which allows them to control the above said process, people have no need to go to institutions which have scope for very limited participation and where results are uncertain. Olson also insists that cooperation is possible only in small groups.[110] In such small groups members know each other, monitor each other, share common benefits and are ready to accept mutual coercion. Participation in decision-making in such groups is fruitful and effective. The Gram Sabha and the village panchayats do not meet the above said requirements. So people prefer to have LCOs which are suitable for their requirements.

Participation in Maintenance of Irrigation Tanks (Kudimaramathu)

The Panchayat Act provides for kudimaramathu but it can not be carried out by the village panchayat or the panchayat union.[111] Scholars like Sengupta[112] and Vani[113] say that kudimaramathu work is being been done in many villages of Tamil Nadu regularly without any outside support by the people themselves. Most of the respondents from both the villages have never participated in any tank maintenance work organised by the panchayat. Practically there is no scope for the panchayats to take the initiative to mobilise the people and collect contributions from them for kudimaramathu. The panchayats are not able to collect even house tax which is ridiculously low. The panchayats are not able to increase house tax to a realistic level. As Jodha has pointed out, the panchayats are not able to "enforce users' obligations."[114] People think that electing panchayat leaders itself is a great contribution. The leaders, keeping elections in mind, are not ready to enforce any obligation.[115] "People only demand and are not ready to contribute anything in return," a panchayat President told the researcher.

As kudimaramathu affects their life, the people of the sudy area perform kudimaramathu without depending on any outside agencies like the panchayats. Ostrom argues that only level users' organisations can sustain the participation of the people in maintaining local resources over a long period and no other agency can sustain such participation.[116] Ostrom gives evidence for such voluntary maintenance work by local communities without any State support.[117] The panchayat unions or village panchayats of Tamil Nadu practically have not taken any initiative in exercising their functions under Section 133 of the Act for kudimaramathu.[118]

Participation in Emergency Maintenance Work

The data collected shows clearly that the LCOs are able to mobilise community participation in protecting tank structures during emergencies like breach of tanks during floods. A scholar on cultural ecology, who studied the tank management of Sivagangai district, says that, because of the nature of the soil (sandy soil) in some parts of Sivagangai area, chances for tank breaches are high.[119] In such topographical context, community care of the tank structure is inevitable. No centralised administrative structure can save tank structures and the community from floods.

In the study area the people are ready to take up the responsibility of saving their tanks without waiting for the panchayat's help. Wade has pointed out the capacity of the local organisations to generate participation at times of risk, which formal organisations do not possess.[120]

Participation in Distribution of Water

Most of the respondents participate in the efforts of the LCOs in the distribution of water from the irrigation tanks to the fields. By taking part in the distribution, the participants ensure that their fields are properly irrigated. They participated in framing rules to ensure that their interests are not affected by the rules of distribution. Ostrom argues that such rules must be framed only at the field level by the affected people.[121] People find that the LCOs are the right type of organisations to facilitate effective participation. By appointing common irrigators, they reduce the transactional cost in terms of wages and time spent on water distribution. The village assembly appoints the common irrigators and fixes their pay. Such decisions are locally made. If the panchayat is involved in the appointment of common irrigators, the procedure will be very complex and expensive. Local arrangements for common irrigators are need based and inexpensive. As per the Act, government officials may regulate the appointment, functioning, and service conditions of the common irrigators. As per the Act common irrigators have to be appointed only by the Revenue Divisional Officer (Deputy Collector). People are wise enough to avoid such complicated procedures and use the local arrangements available to them, which are cheapter and easier to manage.

Participation in Scarcity Management

Most of the respondents in the study villages participate in the LCOs' efforts to manage water scarcity. They have not participated in any such efforts by the panchayats.

Hardin's theory of the tragedy of commons explains the danger of unrestricted use of common resources by users. Users must be rational in using scarce resources to avoid 'Hardin's tragedy'. Only institutions sensitive to the intensity of the problem and its effect on the life of the people are capable of distributing scarce resources prudently. The people of the study area are prudent in the use of water. They are prudent enough to sacrifice a part of their crop to save at least the remaining part in times of water scarcity. In such tight situations people are ready to participate in any effort which is capable of saving their interests. The LCOs, for generations, have been able to manage such situations of scarcity and save people from the risk of crop failure. So people participate in the LCOs' efforts to solve the problem of water scarcity. The LCOs arrange frequent meetings of the village assembly at times of water scarcity. People use the meetings to regularly monitor the water availability and distribution efficiency. They take special efforts to clear field channels to reduce wastage of water. The head end farmers and the tail end farmers are willing to cooperate to use the available water efficiently. In the management of water scarcity local community knowledge (LCK) plays a significant role. The people of Sivagangai district are rich in LCK for management of water scarcity. They have special agronomical techniques and drought resistant varieties of paddy to save them in times of water scarcity.

Another sensitive issue here is the scope for conflicts in sharing of water. It is very high in times of scarcity. The LCOs are purely based on voluntary compliance. So they are better equipped than the panchayats to bring about consensus and avoid conflicts. The panchayats, because of the electoral process, are prone to factionalism and struggle for power. In this context they are not in a position to manage such sensitive issues. Such complex techniques need intensive participation of the community and the panchayats, at present, are not strong enough to take up such type of responsibilities.

Participation in Conservation of Trees and Regulation of Grazing in Village Common Land

Swaminathan sees a village as a watershed community.[122] Without conserving the watershed area the irrigation systems cannot be conserved, used and developed. The degradation of the watershed area may lead to soil erosion, restriction of water flow, siltation of tank bed and reduction in the water holding capacity of the tank. Sukhomajri is a good model of watershed decline as well as watershed development. Due to deforestation, uncontrolled grazing and soil erosion the water bodies there became silted. By restoring the green cover by restricting deforestation and grazing, they could develop well known models of participatory watershed developed.

Most of the respondents in both the villages participate in the efforts of the LCOs in conservation of trees and green cover. They also cooperate with the LCOs' efforts towards regulation of grazing. The study shows that, in spite of their legal powers, the panchayats are not able to attract respondents in the area of conservation of trees and regulation of grazing. The village panchayat Presidents of both the villages admit the role of the LCOs in protecting the trees in the common land. The trees in private lands are also protected by the regulations of the LCOs. Particularly in Pulikanmai village a large number of tamarind trees are found in private lands. Grazing regulations help people to save the trees in private lands too. The panchayats, even though they can legally impose such regulations, are not confident of their ability of enforce such regulations.[123]

As more than 80 per cent of the families in the study area have cultivable land, they are willing to abide by the grazing regulations. They are able to evolve rules among themselves and to impose such restrictions because of the facilitating role of their LCO. Olson's logic of collective action here helps in explaining the capacity of the people to cooperate among themselves to achieve their collective good.[124] Violations of rules related to grazing are collectively monitored and penalised. As Ostrom points out, in self-governing organisations, participatory monitoring by users themselves is more effective than monitoring by any other outside agency.[125] Jodha has also found in his study that the panchayat leaders, who are dependent on the electoral process, may not take the risk of taking unpopular decisions like strict enforcement of rules and punishing violators of the rules.[126]

Participation in the Conservation and Sharing of Fisheries

Most of the respondents from both the villages are actively participating in the efforts of the LCO for the conservation of fisheries in the irrigation tanks and other water bodies in the villages. After the crop harvest, they collectively harvest the fisheries and share the produce among themselves. So far they have not participated in any such efforts initiated by the panchayat for the conservation of fisheries. The Panchayat Act does not have any programme for ensuring people's participation in the development of the fisheries. In fact the panchayats regard the fisheries as a source of revenue. The revenue from the PWD tanks go to the State. The State is not still able to see that the panchayats can use the water bodies to produce fish, a rich food material, for the use of the villagers. The system of public auction of fishing rights in tanks by the panchayats discourages people from developing interest in conserving the fisheries in the irrigation tanks.

The study clearly shows that people's participation is not a pipe dream of academicians but a reality in the field. As Ostrom asserts, in many parts of the world, in small communities, people voluntarily participate for several generations in the management of certain natural resources on which they are critically dependent.

The people of Pulikanmai and Periyakannanur staunchly participate in the management of irrigation tanks and other natural resources. There is a rich social capital in the villages which provides a conducive environment for participation. Environmental condition is a critical variable in the formation of organisational structure in the villages. As there are no other alternative strategies for survival in the form of industry or trade, the people are forced to conserve the available resources. In this context of scarcity and risk, social structure becomes tighter and more cohesive. The village panchayats and the panchayat union in the study area are not able to facilitate people's participation.

As Vani has pointed out, the rules of the panchayats, and, particularly the rules relating to natural resources, are not designed to facilitate people's participation.[127] Most of the rules facilitate State control over the resources. The rules of the panchayats in areas like kudimaramathu are complex and are not easily enforceable. In this context the people of Pulikanmai and Periyakannanur use the LCOs to meet their requirements. All the available indicators show very clearly that, in the perception of the respodents from both the villages, the LCOs facilitate greater participation in the management of the irrigation tanks and other natural resources than the panchayats.

NOTES

1. N.S. Jodha, "Studying Common Property Resources Biography of a Research Project", *Economic and Political Weekly*, March 18, 1995, p. 557.
2. *Ibid.*
3. *Ibid.*
4. *Ibid.*
5. R. Wade, *Village Republic: Economic Conditions for Collective Action in South India*, Bombay: Orient Longman, 1987, pp. 183-187.
6. Cited in Katar Singh, *Managing Common Pool Resources—Principles and Case Studies*, New Delhi: Oxford University Press, 1994, pp. 42-44.
7. R. Wade, *op.cit.*, pp. 152-56.
8. Voluntary Action Network, *State Panchayat Acts: A Critical Review*, New Delhi: VANI 1995, pp. 178-79.
9. *Ibid.*
10. R. Wade, *op.cit.*, p. 203.
11. J.M. Baland, and J.P. Platteau, *Halting Natural Degradation of Natural Resources*, Oxford: Oxford University Press, 1996, pp. 312-343.
12. R. Wade, *op.cit.*, p. 183.
13. N.S. Jodha, "Poverty and Environmental Resource Degradation", *Economic and Political Weekly*, September 5-12, 1998, p. 2383.
14. *Ibid.*
15. N.S. Jodha, "Common Property Resources, A Missing Dimension of Development Strategy", *World Bank Discussion Paper 169*, Washington: World Bank, 1992, p. 36.
16. K. Palanisamy and K. Ramasamy, "Conjunctive Use of Tank and Well Irrigation" J.M. Kern *et al.*, (Eds.), *Natural Resource Economics*, New Delhi: Oxford IBH Publishing Co. Pvt. Ltd., 1997, p. 451.
17. "Illegal quarrying: High Court Orders Recovery", *The Hindu*, Madras: January 14, 1999, p. 4.
18. E. Ostrom, *Crafting Institutions for Self-governing Institutions*, Sansfransisco: Institute for contemporary studies, 1992, pp. 67-69.
19. *Ibid.*, p. 70.
20. *Ibid.*
21. G. Palanithurai, *New Panchayati Raj System at Work: An Evaluation*, New Delhi: Concept Publishing Company, 1998. p. 100.
22. *The Hindu*, Madras: January 14, 1999, *Op.cit.*, p. 4.
23. *Ibid.*
24. R. Wade, *op.cit.*, p. 2.
25. P. Blaikie, J. Harriss and A. Pain, "The Management and Use of Common Property Resources in Tamil Nadu, India" D.W. Bromley (Ed.), *Making Commons Works, Theories, Practice and Policy*, Sanfrancisco: International Centre for Self-Governance, 1992, pp. 254-255.
26. G. Palanithurai, *op.cit.*, p. 203.
27. Cited in Katar Singh, *op.cit.*, pp. 42-44.

28. V. Ragupathy, *Panchayati Raj in Tamil Nadu, One Step Forward and Two Steps Backward*, Gandhigram: PRA Unit, Gandhigram Rural Institute, 1998, pp. 2-4.
29. N.S. Jodha, "Rural Common Property Resources Contributions and Crisis", *Economic and Political Weekly*, June 30, 1990, p. 70.
30. J.C. Pant, "National Policies for Natural Resources Management at Grassroot Level—Overview", *The Indian Journal of Public Administration*, April-June 1998, p. 243.
31. E. Ostrom and O. R. Keohane, *Local Commons and Global Interdependence*, New Delhi: Sage Publication, 1994, pp. 8-12.
32. E. Ostrom, *op.cit.*, p. 70.
33. M.S. Vani, *Role of Panchayat Institutions in Irrigation Management*, New Delhi: The Indian Law Institute, 1992, p. 167.
34. P. Blakie, J. Harriss and A. Pain, *op.cit*, pp. 254-255.
35. G. Palanithurai, *op.cit.*, p. 203.
36. Personal discussion with President Paruthikanmai village panchayat September, 1998.
37. *Ibid.*
38. E. Ostrom and O.R. Keohane, *op.cit.*, p. 16.
39. R. Wade, *op.cit.*, pp. 183-187.
40. R. Palanisamy, R. Balasubramainan, A. Mohmadali, *op.cit.*, p. 46.
41. Robert Chambers, N.C. Saxena, Tushar Shah, *To the Hands of the Poor Water and Trees*, New Delhi: Oxford and IBH Publishing Company Ltd., 1991, pp. 165-166.
42. N.S. Jodha, 1991, *op.cit.*, p. 10.
43. E. Ostrom, *op.cit.*, p. 69.
44. Robert Chambers, N.C. Saxena and Tushar Shah, *op.cit.*, p. 217.
45. E. Ostrom, *op.cit.*, pp. 68-71.
46. *Ibid.*, p. 70.
47. N.S. Jodha, "Poverty and Environmental Resource Degradation", *Economic and Political Weekly*, September, 5-12, 1998, pp. 2835-37.
48. M. Gadgil, "Grassroots Conservation Practices: Revitalising the Traditions" A. Kothari, *et al* (Eds.), *Communities and Conservation*, New Delhi: Sage Publication, 1998, pp. 226-229.
49. E. Ostrom, *op.cit.*, pp. 68-70.
50. Cited in Katar Singh, *op.cit.*, p. 45.
51. Cited in R. Wade, *op.cit.*, p. 2.
52. Voluntary Action Network, *op.cit.*, p. 179.
53. E. Ostrom, *op.cit.*, p. 179.
54. R. Wade, *op.cit.*, pp. 1-18.
55. V. Rengarajan, *Thirukanaper (Tamil)*, Sivagangai: Gnana Peedam Pathipagam, 1998, pp. 141-150.
56. J.M. Baland and J.D. Platteu, *op.cit.*, p. 901.
57. N.S. Jodha, 1990, *op.cit.*, p. 70.
58. E. Ostrom and O.R. Keohane, *op.cit.*, pp. 8-12.

59. Cited in Katar Singh, *op.cit.*, p. 45.
60. K. Palanisamy, R. Balasubramaniam, A. Mohamad Ali, *op.cit.*, p. 6.
61. State Planning Commission, *Report on the Entrustment of Powers to Panchayats*, Government of Tamil Nadu, 1997, p. 45.
62. M.S. Vani, *op.cit.*, pp. 121-123.
63. *Ibid.*
64. E. Ostrom, *op.cit.*, p. 70.
65. Nirmal Sen Gupta, *Managing Common Property: Irrigation in India and Philippines*, New Delhi: Sage Publication. 1991, pp. 76-77.
66. G. Palanithurai, *op.cit.*, pp. 137-139.
67. R. Wade, *op.cit.*, pp. 183-87.
68. Robert Chambers, N.C. Saxena and Tushar Shah, *op.cit.*, pp. 165-166.
69. Group Discussion with Village Panchayat Presidents of Sivagangai District by the Researcher at Gandhigram, August 1998.
70. Robert Chambers. N.C. Saxena and Tushar Shah, *op.cit.*, pp. 167.
71. *Ibid.*
72. K. Chopra, G. Kadikodi. M.N. Murthy, *Participatory Development, People and Common Property Resources*, New Delhi: Sage Publication, 1990, p. 217.
73. N.S. Jodha, "Rural Common Property Resources: A Growing Crisis", *Gate Keeper Series No. 24*, London: International Institute for Environment and Development, 1991.
74. M.S. Vani, *op.cit.*, pp. 166-169.
75. K. Palanisamy, R. Balasubramaniam and A. Mohamad Ali, *op.cit.*, p. 48.
76. *Ibid.*
77. Nirmal Sen Gupta, *op.cit.*, p. 77.
78. *Ibid.*, p. 68.
79. E. Ostrom, *op.cit.*, p. 69.
80. *Ibid.*, p. 71.
81. *Ibid.*
82. Nirmal Sen Gupta, *op.cit.*, p. 104.
83. J.M. Baland and J.P. Platteau, *op.cit.*, p. 92.
84. K. Chopra, G. Kadikodi, M.N. Murthy, *op.cit.*, p. 39.
85. Blaikie Piers, John Harriss and Adam Pain, in Bromley W. Daniel (ed.), *op.cit.*, pp. 254-255.
86. Gnanaprakasam, "Vellai Veechu in Water Management", *Proceedings of National Seminar on Management of Irrigation Tanks*, Madras: Anna University, 1996, pp. 215-217.
87. N.S. Jodha, 1995, *op.cit.*, p. 557.
88. E. Ostrom, *Governing the Commons*, Cambridge: Cambridge University Press, 1990, p. 184.
89. N.S. Jodha, 1998, *op.cit.*, p. 2389.
90. *Ibid.*
91. N.S. Jodha, 1992, *op.cit.*, p. 36.
92. *The Hindu*, Madras: January 14, *op.cit.*, p. 4.

93. E. Ostrom, *op.cit.*, p. 69.
94. N.S. Jodha, 1998, *op.cit.*, p. 2389.
95. *Ibid.*
96. M.S. Vani, *op.cit.*, pp. 167-169.
97. *Ibid.*
98. E. Ostrom, *op.cit.*, pp. 67-69.
99. *Ibid.*
100. Robert Chambers, N.C. Saxena and Tusher Shah, *op.cit.*, pp. 155-59.
101. P. Blaikie, John Harriss and Adam Pain, in Daniel W. Bromley (ed.), *op.cit.*, p. 254.
102. E. Ostrom, *op.cit.*, pp. 69-72.
103. M. Gadgil, R. Guha, *This Fissured land: An Ecological History of India*, New Delhi: Oxford University Press, 1997.
104. E. Ostrom, *op.cit.*, pp. 69-72.
105. *Ibid.*
106. Department of Political Science, *From Participation to Self-governance*, Gandhigram: Gandhigram Rural Institute, 1998, p. 106.
107. J.C. Pant, "National Policies for Natural Resources Management at Grassroot Level—Overview", *The Indian Journal of Public Administration*, April-June 1998, p. 243.
108. G. Palanithurai, *op.cit.*, p. 203.
109. E. Ostrom, *op.cit.*, p. 70.
110. M. Olson, *The Logic of Collective Action: Public Goods and Theory of Groups*, Cambridge: Harvard University Press, 1971, pp. 34-37.
111. State Planning Commission, *op.cit.*, p. 45.
112. Nirmal Sen Gupta, *op.cit.*, p. 77.
113. M.S. Vani, *op.cit.*, p. 139.
114. N.S. Jodha, 1998, *op.cit.*, p. 2389.
115. *Ibid.*
116. E. Ostrom, *op.cit.*, pp. 68-70.
117. *Ibid.*, p. 67.
118. State Planning Commission, *op.cit.*, p. 45.
119. K. Palanisamy, R. Balasubramanian, A. Mohamed Ali, *op.cit.*, p. 33.
120. R. Wade, *op.cit.*, pp. 183-87.
121. E. Ostrom, *op.cit.*, pp. 67-70.
122. Cited in K. Chopra, G. Kadikodi, M.N. Murthy, *op.cit.*, p. 11.
123. N.S. Jodha, 1998, *op.cit.*, p. 2389.
124. Katar Singh, *op.cit.*, p. 32.
125. E. Ostrom, *op.cit.*, p. 71.
126. N.S. Jodha, 1990, *op.cit.*, p. 70.
127. M.S. Vani, *op.cit.*, pp. 166-69.

5

CONCLUSION

Panchayati Raj Institutions have been established at the local level to facilitate people's participation in the development process. In Tamil Nadu, natural resources like irrigation tanks, ponds, grazing lands and unreserved forests are vested with the panchayats. But the panchayats are not able to ensure people's participation in the management of these resources. In some areas of Tamil Nadu, LCOs functioning at the village level are able to facilitate effective people's participation in the management of local natural resources like irrigation tanks without State support.

This study is an attempt to compare the abilities of the panchayats and the LCOs to facilitate people's participation in the management of irrigation tanks. The study was undertaken in an area where irrigation tanks are crucial for the survival of the people. The major findings of the study are given hereunder.

Major Findings

Profile of the Respondents

1. 67 per cent of the respondents from Pulikanmai and 69 per cent of those from Periyakannanur belong to the age group above forty.
2. 90 per cent of respondents from Pulikanmai and 91.80 per cent of those from Periyakannanur are men.
3. 80 per cent of the respondents from Pulikanmai and 70.50 per cent of those from Periyakannanur belong to the BC,

while 20 per cent of the respondents from Pulikanmai and 29.50 per cent of those from Periyakannanur belong to the SC.

4. 70 per cent of the respondents in Pulikanmai are Christians and 30 per cent are Hindus, while 93.44 per cent of the respondents from Periyakannanur are Hindus are 6.55 per cent are Muslims.
5. 90 per cent of the respondents from Pulikanmai and 95 per cent of those from Periyakannanur have agriculture and agricultural employment as their main occupation.
6. In Pulikanmai 20 per cent of the respondents do not hold land. In Periyakannanur all the respondents hold land. Most of the respondents from both the villages are small farmers and have less than 5 acres of land. Only a few have more than 5 acres of land.

Assurance

7. 95 per cent of the respondents from Pulikanmai agree that their interests are not assured by the panchayat and 100 per cent of those from Periyakannanur agree that their interests is not protected by the panchayat.
8. 100 per cent of the respondents from both the study villages say that the panchayats are not able to maintain boundary in the use of irrigation tanks.
9. 95 per cent of the respondents from Pulikanmai and 95.08 per cent of those from Periyakannanur say that the panchayats are not able to give assurance on participant's control over the management of irrigation tanks.
10. None of the respondents from both the study villages think that the panchayats are able to give assurance on their autonomous status.
11. 95 per cent of the respondents from Pulikanmai and 93.44 per cent of those from Periyakannanur do not think that panchayats give assurance on maintaining equity in their transactions.
12. 95 per cent of the respondents from Pulikanmai and 100 per

cent of those from Periyakannanur do not think that the efficiency of the panchayats in the management of irrigation tanks is assured.

13. 90 per cent of the respondents from Pulikanmai and 100 per cent of those from Periyakannanur do not think that the stability of the Panchayati Raj Institutions is assured.
14. 87.50 per cent of the respondents from Pulikanmai and 85.24 per cent of those from Periyakannanur do not think that the adaptability of the panchayats to the changing needs is assured.
15. 87.50 per cent of the respondents from Pulikanmai and 86.88 per cent of those from Periyakannanur do not think that the sustainability of the irrigation tanks is assured by the panchayats.
16. None of the respondents from both the villages think that the transparency and accountability of the transactions of the panchayats is assured.
17. 85 per cent of the respondents from Pulikanmai and 91.80 per cent of those from Periyakannanur think that their interests in irrigation tanks is fully assured by the LCOs.
18. 85 per cent of the respondents from Pulikanmai and 91.80 per cent of those from Periyakannanur think that the LCOs fully assure the proper maintenance of boundary in the use of irrigation tanks.
19. 97.50 per cent of the respondents from Pulikanmai and 90.16 per cent of those from Periyakannanur think that the LCOs fully assure participants' control over the management of irrigation tanks.
20. 82.50 per cent of the respondents from Pulikanmai and 83.60 per cent of those from Periyakannanur think that the autonomy of the LCOs is fully assured.
21. 80 per cent of the respondents from Pulikanmai and 93.44 per cent of those from Periyakannanur feel that the LCOs fully assure equity in their transactions.
22. 85 per cent of the respondents from Pulikanmai and 81.96 per cent of those from Periyakannanur feel that the LCOs fully assure efficiency in the management of irrigation tanks.

23. 95 per cent of the respondents from Pulikanmai and 93.44 per cent of those respondents from Periyakannanur feel assured that the LCOs have organisational stability.
24. 90 per cent of the respondents from Pulikanmai and 95.08 per cent of those from Periyakannanur say that the adaptability of the LCOs is fully assured.
25. 92.50 per cent of the respondents from Pulikanmai and 86.88 per cent of those from Periyakannanur say that the LCOs give full assurance on the sustainable management of the irrigation tanks.
26. 95 per cent of the respondents from Pulikanmai and 83.60 per cent of those from Periyakannanur say that the LCOs fully assure transparency and accountability in their transactions.

Participation

27. 87.50 per cent of the respondents from Pulikanmai and 78.68 per cent of those from Periyakannanur say that they do not participate in the Gram Sabha meetings.
28. More than 90 per cent of the respondents from both the study villages say that they do not influence the decision-making process in the panchayats.
29. 95 per cent of the respondents from Pulikanmai and 93.44 per cent of those from Periyakannaur have never participated in any programme for the maintenance of irrigation tanks facilitated by the panchayats.
30. None of the respondents from both the villages has ever participated in any emergency repair of the irrigation tanks facilitated by the panchayats.
31. None of the respondents from both the villages has ever participated in any programme for the distribution of the water in the irrigation tanks facilitated by the panchayats.
32. None of the respondents from both the villages has ever participated in any effort relating to the management of water scarcity in the irrigation tanks, facilitated by the panchayats.

33. 90 per cent of the respondents from Pulikanmai and 88.52 per cent of those from Periyakannanur have never participated in any effort for the conservation of trees in the village common lands facilitated by the panchayats.
34. None of the respondents from both the villages has ever participated in any effort for regulating grazing in the village common land facilitated by the panchayats.
35. None of the respondents from both the villages has ever participated in any work for the conservation and use of fisheries in the irrigation tanks facilitated by the panchayats.
36. 90 per cent of the respondents from Pulikanmai and 100 per cent of those from Periyakannanur have regularly participated in the village assembly meetings organised by the LCOs.
37. 90 per cent of the respondents from Pulikanmai and 95.08 per cent of those from Periyakannanur participate in the decision-making process of the LCOs.
38. 80 per cent of the respondents from Pulikanmai and 100 per cent of those from Periyakannanur regularly participate in the tank maintenance work facilitated by the LCOs.
39. 90 per cent of the respondents from Pulikanmai and 100 per cent of those from Periyakannanur have regularly participated in emergency repair of the irrigation tanks facilitated by the LCOs.
40. 80 per cent of the respondents from Pulikanmai and 100 per cent of those from Periyakannanur regularly participate in efforts related to water distribution facilitated by the LCOs.
41. 80 per cent of the respondents from Pulikanmai and 100 per cent of those from Periyakannanur regularly participate in the management of water scarcity in the irrigation tanks facilitated by the LCOs.
42. 95 per cent of the respondents from Pulikanmai and 96.72 per cent of those from Periyakannanur regularly participate in the efforts for the conservation of trees facilitated by the LCOs.
43. All the respondents from both the villages participate in the efforts to regulate grazing in the village common lands

facilitated by the LCOs.

44. 90 per cent of the respondents from Pulikanmai and 100 per cent of those from Periyakannanur participate in the efforts to conserve and use the fisheries in the irrigation tanks facilitated by the LCOs.

From the analysis of the available data, the study has come to the following conclusions :

1. In the perception of the people, the LCOs provide better assurance to people than the panchayats in the management of irrigation tanks.
2. In the perception of the people, the LCOs facilitate greater participation of people than the panchayats in the management of panchayat irrigation tanks.

Recommendations on Participatory Management of Natural Resources

Based on the study, the following suggestions are made to facilitate people's participation in the management of natural resources at the grassroot level.

Restoring Ecological Rights of the Community

(i) Most of the laws which were introduced by the British colonial administration to manage natural resources are still in force. The British colonial laws were made to serve the interests of the colonial administration and its industrial and commercial policies. A National Commission on restructuring the laws pertaining to natural resources has to be constituted to recommend new legislation with the objectives of the survival of the people, the sustainability of the resources and the equitable distribution of the resources.

(ii) Wherever possible the management of rural natural resources must be transformed to the Panchayati Raj Institutions along with sufficient powers.

Strengthening the Panchayati Raj System

The 73rd Constitutional Amendment Act, 1992 has to be amended to ensure real devolution of powers from the State Government to the panchayats. If required, a Panchayat List, with specific powers and functions, may be included.

Organic Linkage between Panchayats

Organic linkage between village panchayat, intermediate panchayat and district panchayat must be provided through an indirect system of election beyond the village panchayat.

Extension of Bhuria Committee Recommendations

Some of the recommendations of the Bhuria Committee (Committee appointed by Government of India on Decentralisation of Powers in Scheduled Areas of North Eastern States of India) related to ecological empowerment of the community and constitution of Gram Sabha at the hamlet level may be suitable for non-scheduled areas of the country. The Panchayats (Extension of Scheduled Areas) Act 1996, based on the Bhuria Committee recommendations, gives focus to the ecological empowerment of the community through the panchaysts. Sections of the Act relating to the constitution of the Gram Sabha at the hamlet level and giving the Gram Sabha and the panchayats control over natural resources may be extended to non-scheduled areas also.

Restructuring State Panchayati Raj System in Tamil Nadu

(i) Organic linkage between all the three-tiers must be established.

(ii) All natural resources which fall within a panchayat area must be vested with that particular panchayat. If a particular natural resource can be managed only by a higher level panchayat, that natural resource must be vested with that higher level panchayat.

(iii) Hamlet level assembly of voters or hamlet level sabha must be constituted within the village panchayat with powers to manage water, land and other natural resources.

(iv) No natural resources should be leased out from a panchayat area without getting approval from the hamlet level sabha, Gram Sabha and the panchayat of that area.

(v) No natural resources should be suffered to be extracted for commercial and industrial purposes from a panchayat area by the State or any private organisation without paying due compensation to the panchayat.

Creation of Users' Enterprise within the Panchayati Raj System

To encourage the development and the prudent use of natural resources, the panchayats can permit users' groups, LCOs and cooperative societies to manage natural resources under the panchayat's control.

Local Use of Resources

The maximum possible effort must be made by the panchayats and the State to promote the use of natural resources locally. Local handicrafts and rural industries must be promoted through the supply of raw material at a lower price as an incentive.

Changes in Policies Relating to Irrigation Tanks

(i) The tanks in the rural areas must be under the integrated management of the panchayats on watershed basis. It means that catchment area, tank bed, structures and the command area must be brought under the panchayat's control. The role of the Revenue and the Public Works Departments must be reduced to the minimum.

(ii) Every village must be recognised as a watershed community and village or hamlet level organisations must be empowered and encouraged to manage the watersheds along with the water bodies which fall within the village area.

(iii) Wherever possible LCOs or water users' organisations must be permitted by the panchayats to take over the irrigation tanks on long lease from the panchayats. The panchayats may permit such organisations to function as autonomous bodies accountable to their members. The organisations must function within the legal framework of the panchayats. Reservation must be provided for the Scheduled Caste and women in the executive bodies of such organisations.

(iv) Such organisations may be empowered to collect water charges from the users of the tank water and to ask for contributions in the form of labour of tank maintenance.

(v) The management of usufructs may be vested with these organisations and the income from them may be shared with the panchayat in a mutually agreed upon proportion.

(vi) The organisations must use their income only for the maintenance of the irrigation tank, the development of agriculture and the development of the village. No income from the tank should be shared among its members.

(vii) All the funds under the various development schemes to be spent on the irrigation tank must be routed through the village panchayat to the organisation managing the irrigation tank.

(viii) All the work done by any panchayat in the village watershed area must be approved by the village or hamlet level sabha.

(ix) The hamlet level sabha may have the right to permit the members to collect fuel, fodder and other minor forest products from the village common as per the regulations prescribed by the hamlet level sabha.

(x) The hamlet level sabha may exercise its right to arrange community fishing in the water bodies within the village.

(xii) The State may allot substantial funds for tank modernisation. At least 25 per cent of the total irrigation budget must go to improvement of the tanks as 24 per cent of the total irrigation in the State is tank-based.

Concluding Remarks

The spirit of participation and the organisations that facilitate people's participation are found to exist in varying degrees in villages of Sivagangai district of Tamil Nadu. Participation emerges in situations wherein people face certain crucial problems like drought, water scarcity, crop failure and flood. They motivate people to come together to solve their common problems. In such situations local organisations can facilitate people's participation in collective action for the common good. The local institutions which give sufficient assurance to the participants of meeting their needs are able to ensure participation. The degree to which participation can be facilitated depends on the institutional structure. In this context it needs to be pointed out that the Panchayati Raj Institutions are still not provided with sufficient autonomy to take the responsibility of facilitating people's participation in the management of crucial natural resources like irrigation tanks. The need for involvement of the stake holders in the management of these resources has been asserted by scholars like Ostrom. Here the importance of hamlet level organisations calls for due attention. Local resource enterprises of the people, like users' groups, community organisations and cooperative societies must be encouraged by the panchayats to take up the responsibility of mobilising the people for the management of natural resources. These types of community based institutions can help not only to bring people together but also to gradually overcome the trust gap that exists between people, Panchayat and Government.

The study comes to the optimistic conclusion that there is great potential for participatory management of crucial resources like irrigation tanks in rural areas. This participatory spirit can also be engendered and utilised in other areas of rural development like forestry, fishery, primary education, health, sanitation and employment generation, if appropriate local institutional arrangements are evolved.

APPENDICES

APPENDIX-I

INTERVIEW SCHEDULE

PART-A

Profile of the Respondents

1. Name of the Village :
2. Name of the Respondent :
3. Age :
4. Sex :
5. Community : SC / BC / FC
6. Religion : Hindu/Christian/Muslim/ Others
7. Main Occupation : (a) Agriculture
   (b) Agricultural Employment
   (c) Business
   (d) Government/Organised Sector
   (e) Unorganised Sector.
8. Landholding-wise Distribution (owned or leased)
   (a) Landless.
   (b) Above 1 acre to 2.5 acres.
   (c) Above 2.5 acres to 5 acres.
   (d) Above 5 acres.

PART-B

Assurance

Perception of Assurance Provided by Panchayat

9. Assurance by Panchayats on Protection of Interests.
   (a) Fully assured (b) Fairly assured (c) Not assured
10. Assurance by Panchayats on Maintenance of Boundary.
   (a) Fully assured (b) Fairly assured (c) Not assured
11. Assurance by Panchayats on Participants' Control.
   (a) Fully assured (b) Fairly assured (c) Not assured
12. Assurance by Panchayats on Autonomy.
   (a) Fully assured (b) Fairly assured (c) Not assured
13. Assurance by Panchayats on Equity.
   (a) Fully assured (b) Fairly assured (c) Not assured
14. Assurance by Panchayats on Efficiency.
   (a) Fully assured (b) Fairly assured (c) Not assured
15. Assurance by Panchayats on Stability.
   (a) Fully assured (b) Fairly assured (c) Not assured
16. Assurance by Panchayats on Adaptability.
   (a) Fully assured (b) Fairly assured (c) Not assured
17. Assurance by Panchayats on Sustainability.
   (a) Fully assured (b) Fairly assured (c) Not assured
18. Assurance by Panchayats on Transparency and Accountability.
   (a) Fully assured (b) Fairly assured (c) Not assured

Perception of Assurance Provided by LCOs

19. Assurance by LCOs on Protection of Interests.
   (a) Fully assured (b) Fairly assured (c) Not assured
20. Assurance by LCOs on Maintenance of Boundary.
   (a) Fully assured (b) Fairly assured (c) Not assured
21. Assurance by LCOs on Participants' Control.
   (a) Fully assured (b) Fairly assured (c) Not assured
22. Assurance by LCOs on Autonomy.
   (a) Fully assured (b) Fairly assured (c) Not assured

23. Assurance by LCOs on Equity.
(a) Fully assured (b) Fairly assured (c) Not assured
24. Assurance by LCOs on Efficiency.
(a) Fully assured (b) Fairly assured (c) Not assured
25. Assurance by LCOs on Stability.
(a) Fully assured (b) Fairly assured (c) Not assured
26. Assurance by LCOs on Adaptability.
(a) Fully assured (b) Fairly assured (c) Not assured
27. Assurance by LCOs on Sustainability.
(a) Fully assured (b) Fairly assured (c) Not assured
28. Assurance by LCOs on Transparency and Accountability.
(a) Fully assured (b) Fairly assured (c) Not assured

PART-C

Participation

Participation Facilitated by Panchayats

29. Participation in Gram Sabha Meetings.
(a) Regularly (b) Sometimes (c) Never
30. Participation in Decision-Making Process in the Panchayats.
(a) Regularly (b) Sometimes (c) Never
31. Participation Facilitated by Panchayats in the Maintenance of Irrigation Tanks.
(a) Regularly (b) Sometimes (c) Never
32. Participation Facilitated by Panchayats in the Emergency Repair of Irrigation Tanks.
(a) Regularly (b) Sometimes (c) Never
33. Participation Facilitated by Panchayats in the Distribution of Water.
(a) Regularly (b) Sometimes (c) Never
34. Participation Facilitated by Panchayats in the Management of Water Scarcity.
(a) Regularly (b) Sometimes (c) Never
35. Participation Facilitated by Panchayats in the Conservation of Trees.

(a) Regularly (b) Sometimes (c) Never

36. Participation Facilitated by Panchayats in the Regulation of Grazing.
    (a) Regularly (b) Sometimes (c) Never
37. Participation Facilitated by Panchayats in the Conservation and Use of Fishery in the Irrigation Tanks.
    (a) Regularly (b) Sometimes (c) Never

Participation Facilitated by LCOs

38. Participation in Village Assembly Meetings.
    (a) Regularly (b) Sometimes (c) Never
39. Participation in Decision-Making Process in LCOs.
    (a) Regularly (b) Sometimes (c) Never
40. Participation Facilitated by LCOs in the Maintenance of Irrigation Tanks.
    (a) Regularly (b) Sometimes (c) Never
41. Participation Facilitated by LCOs in the Maintenance of Emergency Repair of Irrigation Tanks.
    (a) Regularly (b) Sometimes (c) Never
42. Participation Facilitated by LCOs in the Distribution of Water.
    (a) Regularly (b) Sometimes (c) Never
43. Participation Facilitated by LCOs in the Management of Water Scarcity.
    (a) Regularly (b) Sometimes (c) Never
44. Participation Facilitated by LCOs in the Conservation of Trees.
    (a) Regularly (b) Sometimes (c) Never
45. Participation Facilitated by LCOs in the Regulation of Grazing.
    (a) Regularly (b) Sometimes (c) Never
46. Participation Facilitated by LCOs in the Conservation and Use of Fishery in the Irrigation Tanks.
    (a) Regularly (b) Sometimes (c) Never

APPENDIX-II

WATERWORKS INDIA*

Name	:	Ganesan
Age	:	57 Years
Village	:	Madaivini Patti
District	:	Madurai
State	:	Tamil Nadu

If you met Ganesan on the street, you will never know that his work requires the skills of a top-of-the-drawer business executive. He manages the water supply of Madaivini Patti, a hamlet on the outskirts of village Vairavan Patti in district Madurai, Tamil Nadu. He is a *neerkatti* (the irrigator in Tamil).

The Chief Ministers of Tamil Nadu and Karnataka will do well to use his water management skills to settle the Cauvery river water dispute. There has never been a major dispute among the farmers of his village regarding water.

Madaivini Patti consists of some 35 families. Poverty, though not abject, is clearly visible. There is only one child who has completed Higher Secondary schooling. In the off-season, the entire village works as casual labour in neighbouring areas.

Agriculture is limited to subsistence. There is hardly any surplus. Paddy is the main crop and water is essential. The only source is the run-off from the monsoon. This travels down the invisible slope of the Eastern Ghats, and collects in the age-old *kanmoy*, as tanks are known here. Effective water management is

* October 15, *Down to Earch*, New Delhi.

crucial to social harmony. Ganesan provides it.

He comes from the *pallar* caste, which is listed as a Scheduled Caste in the State. But there are no special benefits from the government for Ganesan. He lives on what he earns. Which includes the respect of the entire village. His caste status never clouds the recognition and appreciation of his skills. *Pallars* have traditionally managed the water supply in this area.

At all community functions, the village priests have to accompany Ganesan to the market to make purchases, a symbol of his special status. He is the authoritative mediator, the honest broker, the village elder. In not just the water disputes but even the social disagreements within the village.

Says S. Subramaniam, executive committee member of the village's Tanks Farmer's Association: "The *neerkatti* tradition is of great benefit. Faith in the *neerkatti* is crucial to the smooth functioning of agriculture. Otherwise everyone will fight".

Ganesan knows the topography of the village like the palm of his hand. He knows exactly where the water comes from and where it should go. He knows the water need of each and every farmer, each and every crop. His work starts before the monsoon. He walks through the channels, digging and clearing in rhythmical motion. Singing a song or two.

Then there is the maintenance of the embankments of the *kanmoy*. But the most crucial part is the operation of the wooden sluice valves that release water in the channels. This is where the fate of all the farmers rests. While operating the valves, Ganesan is dealing with the life-blood of the village economy. One mistake in the calculation of waterflow and timing of the valves can ruin a poor farmer's crop. Yet it never happens.

Ganesan's social status apart, his economic condition is no better than the rest of the village. For maintaining the channels and the *kanmoy*, he receives rice from each farmer in proportion to the size of the fields (4.5 kg of rice per 60 cents of crop area). In addition, he gets 4 kg of rice from each farmer for operating the sluice valves. If he requires an additional hand or two in his endeavours, it is his own headache.

However, work in the village is restricted to the monsoon. That, too, once in three years. He has two brothers who are also *neerkattis*. They take up water management in turns.

In the off-season, Ganesan has to go looking for daily wages to either the neighbouring fields as agricultural labour or to the nearby towns as a loader. Some days are good. He manages to earn Rs. 50. Others are bad.

Ganesan's two sons and four daughters are not interested in carrying on the *neerkatti* tradition. But as long as there are paddy fields, the limited water will need to be managed with care. There will have to be a *neerkatti*. A tradition.

GLOSSARY

Boundary	Restriction of the use of a particular resource to specific persons under specific regulations.
Common Irrigator	A person responsible for irrigation in the tank irrigated area appointed by the Local Community Organisation (LCO) and functioning under the LCO.
Common Property	A property owned or used in common by an identifiable group of people who have claim over its use. Village grazing pastures, forest and irrigation tanks are typical common property resources in rural India.
Field Channel	The water channel taking water from the tank to the fields.
Free Rider	A person enjoying a benefit from a common good realised out of others' contribution, without himself contributing.
Irrigation Tank	A small reservoir constructed across a slope of the valley to catch and store water during rainy season to be used for irrigation in dry season.
Kudi	Family residing in the village and having membership in the LCO of the village.
Kudimaramathu	Maintenance and repair work done in an irrigation tank by the local community.
Poramboke Land	Land which is owned by the State and vested with the panchayats. Grazing

	grounds, waste lands and threshing floors are some of the poramboke lands in rural India.
Open Access Resource	A resource which is accessible to everybody and whose use is not regulated by any rules, regulations and conventions, etc.
Ryotwari	A revenue settlement made with the actual cultivator by the State.
Sluice	Outlet point in a tank through which water is distributed to the fields.
Supply Channel	The water channel bringing rain water to the irrigation tank.
Surplus Weir	A tank structure permitting overflow of excess water from the tank.
Watershed	Drainage base of a stream. Irrigation tanks get water from their watersheds.

BIBLIOGRAPHY

Agarwal, A. and S. Narain, *Towards Green Villages*, Delhi: Centre for Science and Environment, 1989.

——, *Dying Wisdom*, New Delhi: Centre for Science and Environment, 1997.

Agarwal, B., "Social Security and Family: Coping with Seasonality and Calamity in Rural India", E.J. Ahmad, *et al.* (Eds.), *Social Security in Developing Countries*, Oxford: Clarendon Press, 1991.

Allen, R., *Enclosures and the Yeomen*, Oxford: Oxford University Press, 1992.

Badcock, C.R., *The Problems of Altruism-Freudian-Darwinian Solutions*, Oxford: Black Well, 1986.

Baland, J.M. and J.P. Plateau, *Halting Natural Degradation of Natural Resources*, Oxford: Oxford University Press, 1996.

Banerjee, U., "People's Participation: A New Concept in Development", *Vacham*, Vol. V. No. 2, April, 1994.

Bandyopadhyay, J. and V. Siva, "Chipco: Rekindling India's Forest Culture", *The Ecologist*, 17/1: 1987.

Berkes, F., "Local-level Management and the Common Problems: A Comparative Study of Turkish Coastal Fisheries", *Marine Policy*, 10th July, 1986.

Berkes, F. (Ed.), *Common Property Resources: Ecology and Community-Based Sustainable Development*, New York: Belhaven Press, 1989.

Bhargava, B.S., *Emerging Leadership in Panchayati Raj System*, Bangalore: Institute of Social and Economic Change, 1977.

Bhargava, B.S., *Panchayati Raj System and Political Parties*, New Delhi: Ashish Publishing House, 1979.

Bhargava, B.S. and S. Rama Rao, *Indian Local Government: A*

Study, Calcutta: Minerva Associates, 1978.

Bhargava, B.S. and V. Vengatakrishnan, "Panchayati Raj System in Tamil Nadu—Some Issues and Problems", *Kurukshetra*, Vol. XLI, No. 4, January, 1993.

Bhagava, B.S. and C. Raphael, Jos, "Working of Gram Sabhas in Karnataka: A Study at Micro Level", *Journal of Rural Development*, Vol. 13, No. 2, April-June, 1994.

Blaikie, Piers, John Harris and Adam Pain, "The Management and Use of Common Property Resource in Tamil Nadu, India", Bromley W. Daniel (Eds.), *Making the Commons Work: Theories and Practices*, Sanfrancisco: International Centre for Self Governance, 1992.

Blair, W. Harry, "Democracy, Equity and Common Property Resource Management in Indian Sub-continent" in *Development and Change*, Vol. 27, 1996.

Block Panchayat Office, *Kalayar Kovil Block Profile*, Kalayar Kovil: Block Panchayat Office, 1998.

Block Panchayat Office, *Local Irrigation Tank Register*, Kalayar Kovil: Block Panchayat Office, 1998.

Bob Sam, "Tragedy of Common", *Journal of Rural Development*, Vol. 17(1), 1998.

Brara, R., *Shifting Sands: A Study of Rights in Common Pastures*, Jaipur: Institute of Development Studies, 1987.

Broad, R., "The Poor and the Environment: Friends or Foes?", *World Development* 22/6, 1994.

Cernea, M.M., "User Groups as Producers in Participatory Afforestation Strategies", *World Bank Discussion Papers*, No. 70, Washington, DC: World Bank, 1989.

Chambers, Robert, N.C. Saxena, Tushar Shah, *To the Hands of the Poor Water and Trees*, New Delhi: Oxford and IBH Publishing Company Ltd., 1991.

Chand, R., "Role of Water Rights in Farmer-Managed Hill Irrigation Systems", *Economic and Political Weekly*, 29/13, 1994.

Chopra, K., G. Kadikodi and M.N. Murthy, *Participatory Development, People and Common Property Resources*, New Delhi: Sage Publication, 1990.

Dharampal, *Indian Science and Technology in the Eighteenth Century*, Delhi: Impex India, 1971.

——, *The Madras Panchayat System Vol. II, General Assessment*, Delhi: Impex India, 1973.

Department of Political Science, *From Participation to Self-Governance*, Gandhigram: Gandhigram Rural Institute, 1998.

Desai, V., *Rural Development*, New Delhi: Himalaya Publishing House, 1988.

District Collector Office, *District Resource Survey Profile*, Sivagangai: Collector Office, 1997.

District Rural Development Agency, *District Profile*, Sivagangai: District Rural Development Agency, 1998.

Gadgil, M., "Grassroots Conservation Practices: Revitalising the Traditions", A. Kothari, *et al.* (Eds.), *Communities and Conservation*, New Delhi: Sage Publication, 1998.

Gadgil, M. and R. Guha, "Ecological Conflicts and the Environmental Movement in India", *Development and Change*, 25/1, 1994.

——, *This Fissured Land: An Ecological History in India*, New Delhi: Oxford University Press, 1997.

Gibbs, J.N., Christopher and Bromely W. Daniel, "Institutional arrangements for Management of natural resources: Common Property Regimes", Firket Berkes (Ed.), *Common Property Resources*, Dehradun: International Book Distributors, 1991.

Gnanaprakasam, "Vellai Veechu in Water Management", *Proceedings of National Seminar on Water Management*, Madras: Anna University, 1996.

Gomathinayagam, "Palanthamilar Pasana Perumai", *Dinamani Pongal Malar (Tamil)*, Madras, 1998.

Government of India, *The Constitution of India*, New Delhi: Government Publication, 1996.

Government of Madras, *Madras Panchayat Act, 1920*, Madras: Government Publication, 1920.

Government of Madras, *Madras Panchayat Act, 1958*, Madras: Government Publication, 1958.

Government of Tamil Nadu, *Tamil Nadu Panchayat Act, 1994*, Madras: Government Publication, 1994.

Gupta, A.K., "Why Poor do not Cooperate: Lessons from Modern

Organisation", M. Clare, G. Wanger (Eds.) *Research Relationships Politics and Practice of Social Research*, London: G.C. George Allen and Unwin, 1987.

Hardin, G., "The Tragedy of Commons", *Science* 162, 1968.

Hardin, G. and J. Baden (Eds.), *Managing the Commons*, San-francisco: W.H. Freeman & Co., 1977.

Harichandran, *Panchahati Raj and Rural Development: A Study of Tamil Nadu*, New Delhi: Concept Publishing Company, 1983.

Janakarajan, S., "In Search of Tanks: Some Hidden Facts", *Working Paper No. 97*, Madras: Madras Institute of Development Studies, 1991.

Jodha, N.S., "Rural Common Property Resources Contributors and Crisis", *Economic and Political Weekly*, June 30, 1990.

——, "Rural Common Property Resources: A Growing Crisis", *Gate Keeper Series No. 24*, London: International Institute for Environment and Development, 1991.

——, "Common Property Resources: A Missing Dimension of Development Strategy", *World Bank Discussion Paper 169*, Washington: World Bank, 1992.

——, "Studying Common Property Resources Biography of a Research Project", *Economic and Political Weekly*, March 18, 1995.

——, "Poverty and Environmental Resource Degradation", *Economic and Political Weekly*, September 5-12, 1998.

Krishnan, P.J., "Legal and Policy Issues in Community based Conservation", A. Kothari, *et al.* (Eds.), *Communities and Conservation*, New Delhi: Sage Publication, 1998.

LCO, *Pulikanmai LCO Accounts Book 1977*, Pulikanmai: LCO, 1977.

LCO, *Pulikanmai LCO Accounts Book 1988-89*, Pulikanmai: LCO, 1989.

LCO, *Pulikanmai LCO Accounts Book 1996-97*, Pulikanmai: LCO, 1997.

LCO, *Kudi Register*, Pulikanmai: LCO, 1998.

LCO, *Kudi Register*, Periyakannanur: LCO, 1998.

Lewis, D.K., *Convention: A Philosophical Study*, Cambridge: Harvard University Press, 1969.

Liela, Narayanan, "Tank Management Change and Continuity, Rejuvenation and Extension of Traditional System", *Proceedings of National Seminar on Management of Irrigation Tanks*, Madras: Anna University, 1996.

Malik, Madhushree and S.N. Sangita, "Local Organisations, Common Property Land Resources and Rural Poor", *Waste Land News*, Feb.-April, 1993.

Mathew, George, *Panchayati Raj: From Legislation to Movement*, New Delhi: Concept Publishing Company, 1994.

Mitra, A.K., "Joint Management of Irrigation Systems in India: Relevance of Japanese Experience", *Economic and Political Weekly*, 27-26, 1992.

Moloney, C. and K.V. Raju, *Managing Irrigation Together*, New Delhi: Sage Publications, 1994.

Monoharan, M., *Maruthupandia Mannargal (Tamil)*, Sivagangai: Annam Publishers, 1994.

Mosse, David, *Local Institutions, Ecology and History in South Indian Tank Irrigation System*, Swansea: Centre for Development Studies, University of Wales, 1996.

Mukherji, R.K., "Natural Resource Management Lessons from Indian Experiments", *Waste Land News*, Nov. 94, Jan. 95.

Norman, Uphoff, "Local Institutions and Participation for Sustainable Development", *Gate Keeper Series, No. 31*, London: International Institute for Environment and Development, 1992.

Olson, M., *The Logic of Collective Action: Public Goods and the Theory of Groups*, Cambridge: Harvard University Press, 1971.

Ostrom, E., *Governing the Commons: Evolution of Institutions for Collective Action*, New York: Cambridge University Press, 1990.

——, *Crafting Institutions for Self-Governing Institutions*, Sansfransisco: Institute for Contemporary Studies, 1992.

Ostrom, E. and O.R. Keohane, *Local Commons and Global Interdependence*, New Delhi: Sage Publications, 1994.

Palanisami, K., R. Balasubramanian and A. Mohammed Ali, *Present Status and Future Strategies of Tank Irrigation in Tamil*

Nadu, Coimbatore: Tamil Nadu Agricultural University, 1997.

Palanisami, K. and K. Ramasamy, "Conjunctive Use of Tank and Well Irrigation", J.M. Kern, *et al.*, (Eds.), *Natural Resource Economics*, New Delhi: Oxford IBH Publishing Co. Pvt. Ltd., 1997.

Palanithurai, G., *Empowering People Participation: A Study in New Panchayati Raj System*, New Delhi: Kanishka Publishing House, 1994.

——, (Ed.), *New Panchayati Raj System: Status and Prospects*, New Delhi: Kanishka Publishing House, 1995.

——, (Ed.), *Empowering People: Issues and Solutions*, New Delhi: Kanishka Publishing House, 1996.

——, *Perception of Grassroot Democracy and Evaluation of Political Performance*, New Delhi: MD Publications, 1997.

——, *Major Issues in New Panchayati Raj System*, New Delhi: Kanishka Publishing House, 1997.

——, *New Panchayati Raj System at Work: An Evaluation*, New Delhi: Concept Publishers, 1999.

Pant, J.C., "National Policies for Natural Resource Management at Grassroot Level—Overview", *The Indian Journal of Public Administration*, Vol. XLIV: No. 2, April-June, New Delhi, 1998.

Pugalendhi, S., *Uratchigal, Peruratchigal, Uratchi Onriumgal Sattamum Nadaimuraiyum (Tamil)*, Madras: Poongodi Publishers, 1990.

Ragupathy, V., "A Survey on Kudi System in Sivagangai District Tamil Nadu", *Unpublished Report*, Gandhigram: Department of Political Science and Development Administration, Gandhigram Rural Institute, 1998.

——, *Panchayati Raj in Tamil Nadu, One Step Forward and Two Steps Backward*, Gandhigram: PRA Unit, Gandhigram Rural University, 1998.

Rengarajan, V., *Thirukanaper (Tamil)*, Sivagangai: Gnana Peedam Pathipagam, 1998.

Runge, C.F., "Common Property Externalities; Isolation, Assurance and Resource Depletion in a Traditional Grazing Context", *American Journal of Agricultural Economics*, 66/5, 1981.

——, "Institutions and Free Ridder; the assurance problem in collective action", *The Journal of Politics*, 46/1, 1984.

Saraswathy, S., *The Madras Panchayat System: Vol. I, A Historical Survey*, Delhi: Impex India, 1973.

Sasikanth, "Gandhian Approach to Management of Forest as a Common Property Resource: A Case Study of Binj Giri Hills in Orissa, India", *Paper Presented in the First International Conference on Common Property Resources*, Durham: Duke University, 1990.

Sekar, Madhushree, "Organisation for Sustainable Common Property Resource Development", *Review of Development and Change*, 11/1, January-June, 1997.

Sengupta, Nirmal, *Managing Common Property: Irrigation in India and Philippines*, New Delhi: Sage Publications, 1991.

Shubik, M., *Game Theory in the Social Science: Concepts and Solutions*, Cambridge: MIT Press, 1982.

Singh, Katar, *Peoples Participation in Natural Resource Management*, Anand: Institute of Rural Management, 1992.

——, *Management of Common Pool Resources—Principles and Case Studies*, New Delhi: Oxford University Press, 1994.

Staff Reporter, "Illegal Quarrying: High Court Orders Recovery", *The Hindu*, Madras: January 14, 1999.

State Planning Commission, *Report on the Entrustment of Powers to Panchayats*, Government of Tamil Nadu, 1998.

University of Madras, *Tamil Lexicon*, Madras, 1982.

Vani, M.S., *Role of Panchayat Institutions in Irrigation Management*, New Delhi: The Indian Law Institute, 1992.

Village Administrative Office, *Irrigation Tank Record*, Pulikanmai: Village Administrative Office, 1998.

——, *Irrigation Tank Record*, Periyakannanur: Village Administrative Office, 1998.

Village Panchayat, *Minutes of the Purithikanmai Village Panchayat Meetings 1996-97*, Paruthikanmai: Village Panchayat, 1997.

——, *Paruthikanmai Village Panchayat Quarterly Report*, Paruthikanmai: Village Panchayat, December, 1997.

——, *Paruthikanmai Village Panchayat Income and Expenditure Statement 1996-97 and 1997-98*, Paruthikanmai : Village

Panchayat, 1998.

——, *Periyakannanur Village Panchayat Quarterly Report*, Periyakannanur : Village Panchayat, December, 1996.

——, *Periyakannanur Village Panchayat Income and Expenditure Statement 1997-98*, Periyakannanur : Village Panchayat, 1998.

——, *Periyakannanur Village Panchayat Quarterly Report*, Periyakannanur : Village Panchayat, March, 1998.

——, *Periyakannanur Village Panchayat Quarterly Report*, Periyakannanur : Village Panchayat, December, 1998.

Voluntary Action Network, *State Panchayat Acts: A Critical Review*, New Delhi: Vani 1995.

Wade, R., *Village Republic: Economic Conditions for Collective Action in South India*, Bombay: Orient Longman, 1987.

INDEX